ROBERT JOHN

GUNS N' ROSES
USE YOUR ILLUSION II

Management: Doug Goldstein/Big F D Entertainment, Inc.
Edited by Steve Gorenberg, Kerry O'Brien, Andy Aledort and Jon Chappell
Music Engraving by W.R. Music
Production Manager: Daniel Rosenbaum
Art Direction: Kerstin Fairbend
Director Of Music: Mark Phillips
Cover Painting: Mark Kostabi

ISBN: 0-89524-687-2

GUNS N'

GENE KIRKLAND

GENE KIRKLAND

USE YOUR

ROSES

ROBERT JOHN

ROBERT JOHN

ILLUSION II

GENE KIRKLAND

Contents

FULL COLOR FOLD-OUT FOLLOWS PAGE 16

TABLATURE EXPLANATION

TABLATURE: A six-line staff that graphically represents the guitar fingerboard, with the top line indicating the highest sounding string (high E). By placing a number on the appropriate line, the string and fret of any note can be indicated. The number 0 represents an open string.

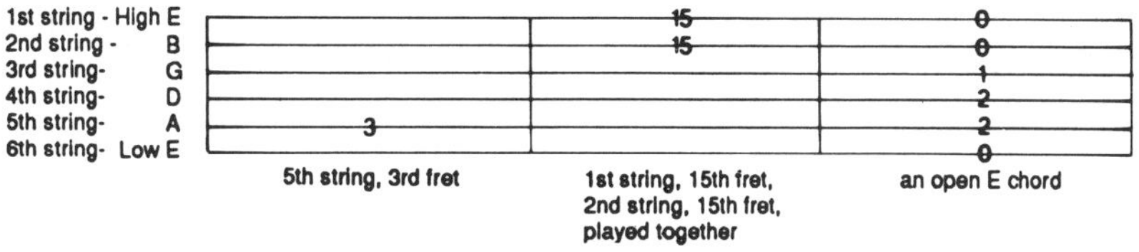

Definitions for Special Guitar Notation

BEND: Strike the note and bend up ½ step (one fret).

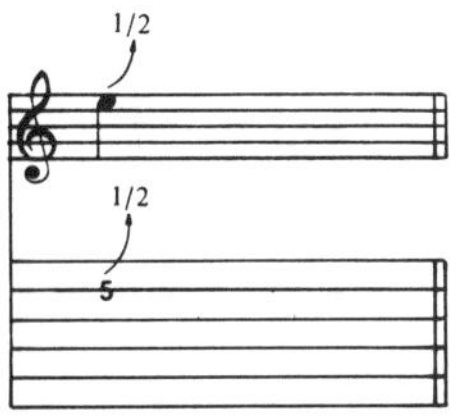

BEND: Strike the note and bend up a whole step (two frets).

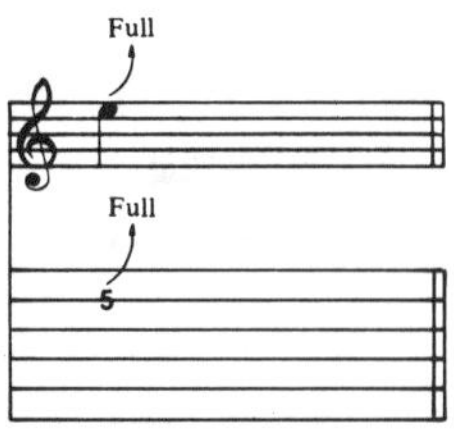

BEND AND RELEASE: Strike the note and bend up ½ (or whole) step, then release the bend back to the original note. All three notes are tied, only the first note is struck.

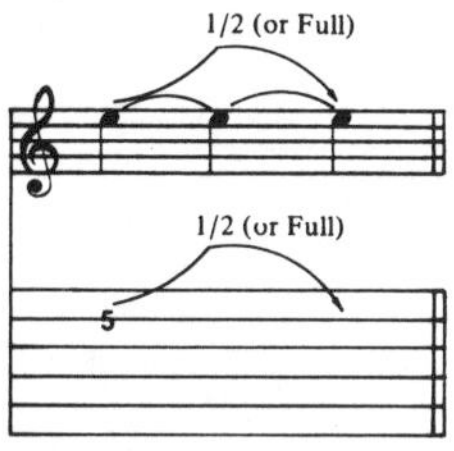

PRE-BEND: Bend the note up ½ (or whole) step, then strike it.

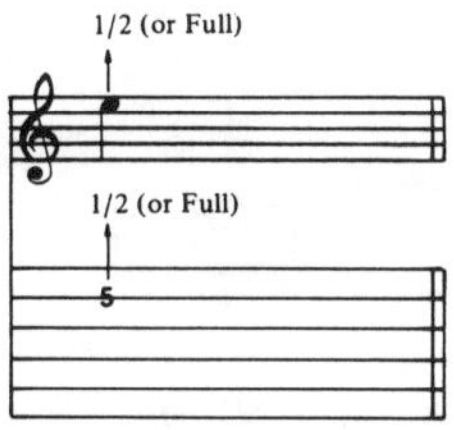

PRE-BEND AND RELEASE: Bend the note up ½ (or whole) step. Strike it and release the bend back to the original note.

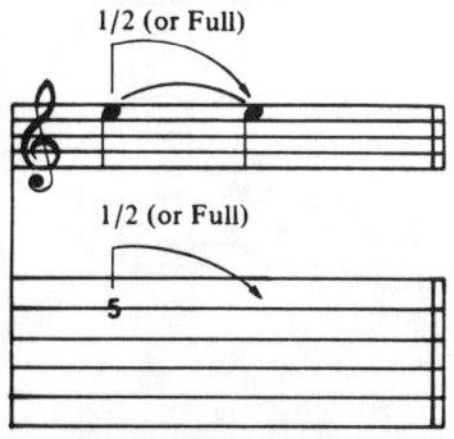

UNISON BEND: Strike the two notes simultaneously and bend the lower note up to the pitch of the higher.

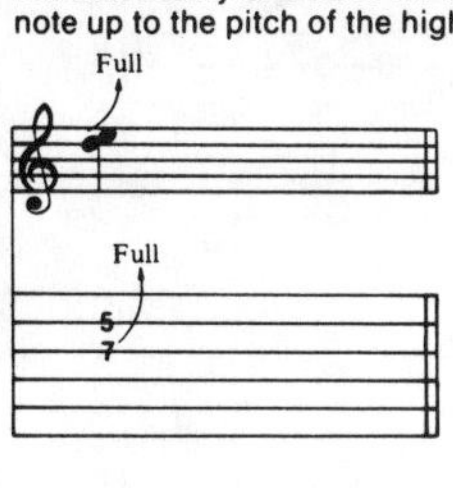

VIBRATO: The string is vibrated by rapidly bending and releasing the note with the left hand or tremolo bar.

WIDE OR EXAGGERATED VIBRATO: The pitch is varied to a greater degree by vibrating with the left hand or tremolo bar.

SLIDE: Strike the first note and then slide the same left-hand finger up or down to the second note. The second note is not struck.

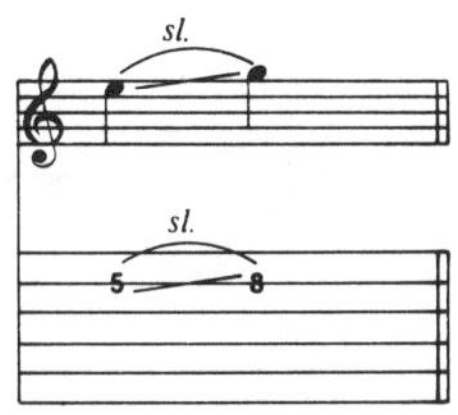

SLIDE: Same as above, except the second note is struck.

HAMMER-ON: Strike the first (lower) note, then sound the higher note with another finger by fretting it without picking.

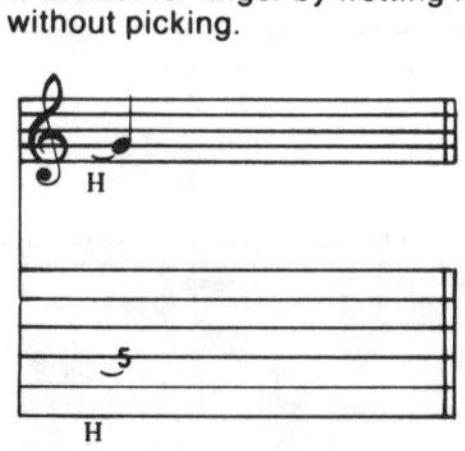

PULL-OFF: Place both fingers on the notes to be sounded. Strike the first note and without picking, pull the finger off to sound the second (lower) note.

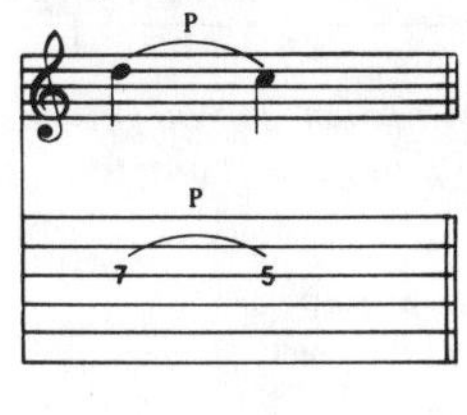

TRILL: Very rapidly alternate between the note indicated and the small note shown in parentheses by hammering on and pulling off.

TAPPING: Hammer ("tap") the fret indicated with the right-hand index or middle finger and pull off to the note fretted by the left hand.

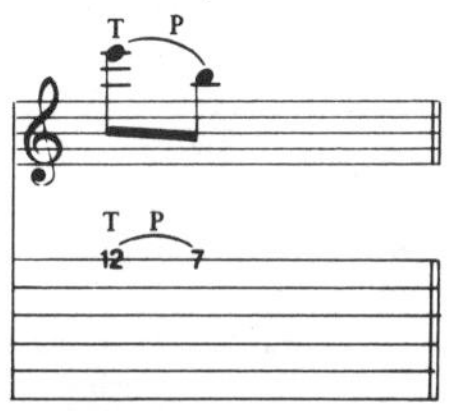

PICK SLIDE: The edge of the pick is rubbed down the length of the string producing a scratchy sound.

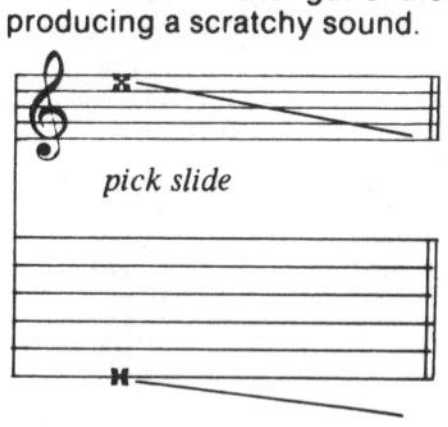

TREMOLO PICKING: The note is picked as rapidly and continuously as possible.

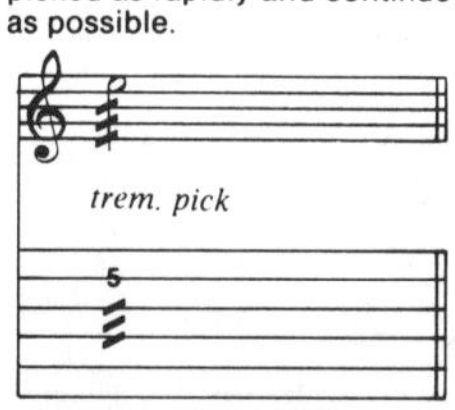

NATURAL HARMONIC: Strike the note while the left hand lightly touches the string over the fret indicated.

ARTIFICIAL HARMONIC: The note is fretted normally and a harmonic is produced by adding the edge of the thumb or the tip of the index finger of the right hand to the normal pick attack. High volume or distortion will allow for a greater variety of harmonics.

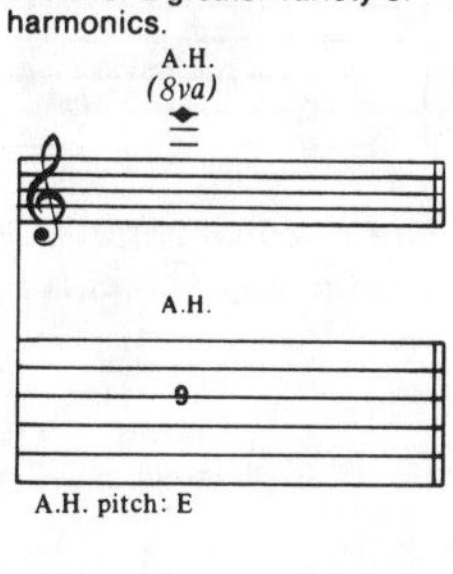

TREMOLO BAR: The pitch of the note or chord is dropped a specified number of steps then returned to the original pitch.

PALM MUTING: The note is partially muted by the right hand lightly touching the string(s) just before the bridge.

MUFFLED STRINGS: A percussive sound is produced by laying the left hand across the strings without depressing them and striking them with the right hand.

RHYTHM SLASHES: Strum chords in rhythm indicated. Use chord voicings found in the fingering diagrams at the top of the first page of the transcription.

RHYTHM SLASHES (SINGLE NOTES): Single notes can be indicated in rhythm slashes. The circled number above the note name indicates which string to play. When successive notes are played on the same string, only the fret numbers are given.

CIVIL WAR

(Special Thanks Niven/James)

Words and Music by
Slash, Duff McKagan
and W. Axl Rose

*Recitation: "What we've got here is... failure to communicate. Some men you just can't reach, so you get what we had here last week, which is the way he wants it. Well, he gets it! N' I don't like it any more than you men."

Chorus
(All gtrs.)
Em C D G5 B5 A
ev-'ry-bod-y's fight-in' their the prom-ised land, and
I don't need your civ-il war.
E5 G5 B5 A E5 CIII DV
It feeds the rich while it bur-ies the poor.
G5 B5 E5 E E5
Your pow-er hun-gry sell-in' sol-diers in a hum-an gro-c'ry store, ain't that fresh!
2nd time to Coda
G5 B5 A E5 CIII DV
I don't need your Civ-il War. Oo, no, no, no, no, no!
Guitar solo
G B5 E5 G B5
Gtr. II
hold bend
(w/wah wah)
*Two gtrs. arr. for one gtr.
E5 CIII DV G B5 E5
P.M.

3rd Verse
*w/Rhy. Fig. 1 (2 times)
G B5 E5 C III D V E5
Look at the shoes_ you're fill - ing.
dim.
*Doubled by elec. gtr.
G Em G D/F♯
Look at the blood_ we're spill - ing. Look at the world_ we're kill - ing the way we've al - ways done be - fore._
Em G
Look in the doubt_ we've wal - lowed. Look at the lead - ers we've fol - lowed. Look at the lives_ we've swal - lowed and
Gtr. II
mf
w/Riff B
*A5(type 2)
A5♯4 A5
4th Verse
w/Rhy. Figs. 2 & 2A
G D/F♯ E5
I don't want to hear_ no more._ My hands_ are tied._ For
*Two gtrs. arr. for one gtr.
G D/F♯ E5
all I've seen_ has changed_ my mind,_ but still the wars_ go on_ as the years_ go by_ with no
⑥ open 3fr. 7fr.
G D E G F♯ E5
w/Rhy. Fill 1
G
love of God_ or hu - man rights._ 'Cause all_ these dreams are swept_ a - side_ by blood - y hands_ of the hyp - no - tized_ who

*Recitation: "We practice selective annihilation of mayors and government officials. For example, to create a vacuum. Then we fill that vacuum, as popular war advances. Peace is closer."

D.S. al Coda
N.C.(D/A)
F/A
Am
C5
Full
sl.
Double time ♩ = 144
Coda
E5
CIII
DV
Rhy. Fig. 4
G
B5
no, no, no, no, no, no, no, no, no, no, no, no, no! I don't need your civ-il war!
*Two gtrs. arr. for one gtr.
④open
D
I don't need your civ-il war!
sim.
Your pow-er hun-gry sell-in' sol-diers in a hu-man gro-c'ry store, ain't that fresh!
(end Rhy. Fig. 4)
I don't need your civ-il war, no no no no no no no. no, ah, no, ah,
...war.
Outro solo
w/Rhy. Fig. 4
no! I don't need one more war!
1/2
f (w/wah wah)

G
B5
E5
oh, — whoa!
C III
D V
G
B5
E5
8va
G
B5
E5
Oo, I don't need one more war, no no no
8va

Half time ♩ = 72
C^III
D^V
G
N.C.
no,— ah, no,— ah, no.
rit.
8va
loco
Full
mf
(w/wah wah)
sl. sl. sl.
P
w/Rain & thunder
(Spoken) Whaz so civ - il 'bout war, an - y - way?
(Whistled melody arr. for gtr.)
Begin fade
Fade out

ROBERT JOHN

Cherry Lane Music

14 YEARS

Words and Music by
Izzy Stradlin' and W. Axl Rose

w/Rhy. Fig. 1 (2 times - Gtr. I)
(F5)
(E5)
Am
G
with your com - plaints..
You cry and moan and com - plain,
*Gtr. II
(end Rhy. Fig. 1)
P.M.
P.M.
H
Play 1st time only
*2nd & 3rd times Gtr. II doubles Gtr. I.
F
N.C.(E5)
Am
G
you whine and tear.
Up to my neck in sor - row,
F
N.C.(E5)
Rhy. Fig. 2 (Gtr. I)
Pre-chorus
A5
C
the touch you bring..
You just don't step in - side to,
Rhy. Fig. 2A (Gtr. II)

(end Rhy. Fig. 2)
w/Rhy. Figs. 2 & 2A (3 times)
D
A5
C
to four - teen years...
So hard to keep my own head...
(end Rhy. Fig. 2A)
7 7 7 5
(7 7 7 5)
D
A5
C
that's what I say and you know...
I've been the beg - gar...
3rd time to Coda
D
A5
C
I've played the thief...
I was the dog...
Chorus
Gtrs. I & II
D
A5
G5
they all tried to beat.
But it's been four - teen years of si - lence. It's been
D/A
A5
G5
four - teen years of pain.
It's been four - teen years that are gone for - ev - er and I'll
1
D/A
w/Rhy. Fig. 1 (2 times - Gtrs. I & II)
N.C.(A5)
(G5)
nev - er have a - gain, well.
(F5)
(E5)
(A5)
(G5)
2
D/A
(F5)
(E5)
nev - er have a - gain, well.

Guitar solo
A5
G5
D/A
Gtrs. I & II
Gtr. III
semi-harm.
C
D
Full
1½
H
P
sl.

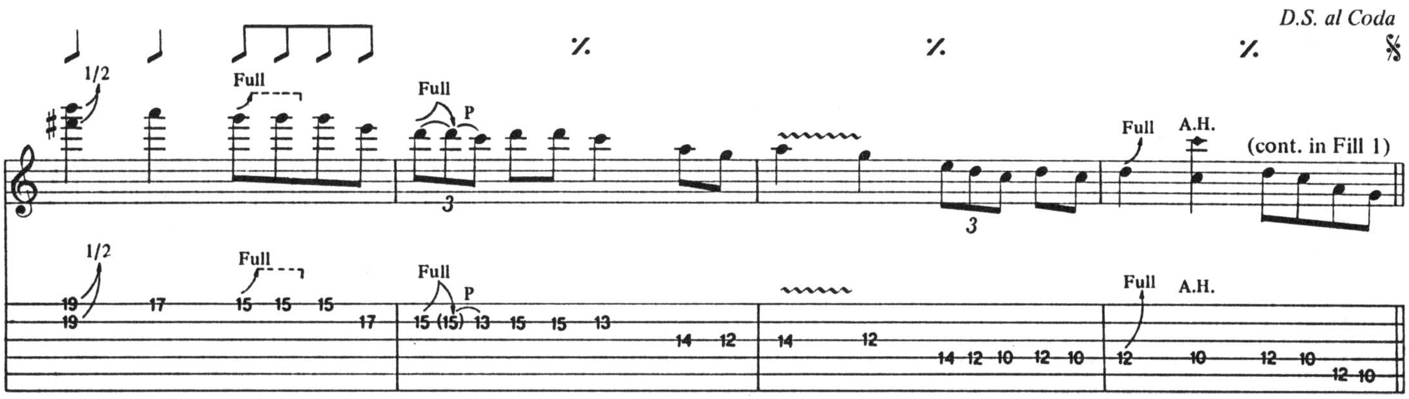

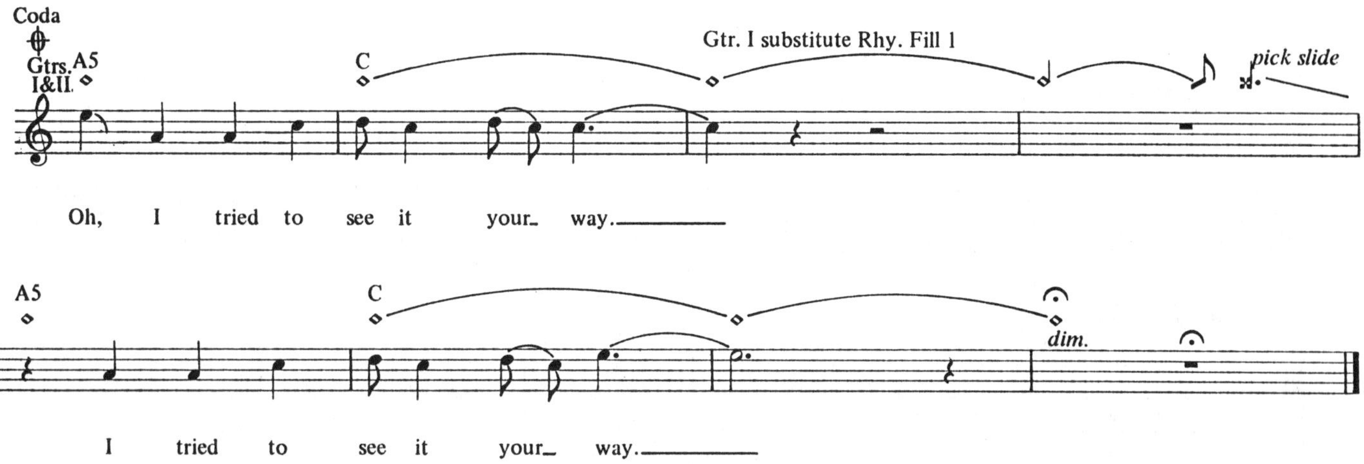

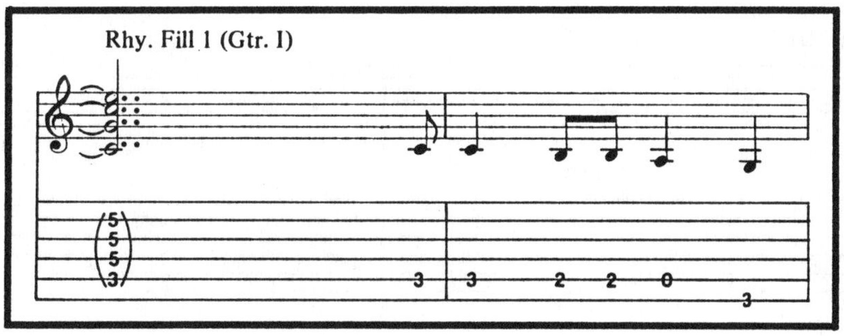

Additional Lyrics

2. Your stupid girlfriends tell you that I'm to blame.
Well, they're all used-up has-beens, out of the game.
This time I'll have the last word, you hear what I say?
I tried to see it your way, it won't work today.

2nd Pre-chorus:
You just don't step inside to 14 years.
So hard to keep my own head... that's what I say.
You know... I've been the dealer... hangin' on your street.
I was the dog... they all tried to beat. *(To Chorus)*

3. Bullshit and contemplation, gossip's their trade.
If they knew half the real truth, what would they say?
Well, I'm past the point of concern, it's time to play.
These last 4 years of madness sure put me straight.

3rd Pre-chorus:
Don't get back 14 years in just one day.
So hard to keep my own head. Just go away.
You know... just like a hooker, she said, "Nothin's for free."
Oh, I tried to see it your way.
I tried to see it your way.

YESTERDAYS

Words and Music by
West Arkeen, Del James,
Billy and W. Axl Rose

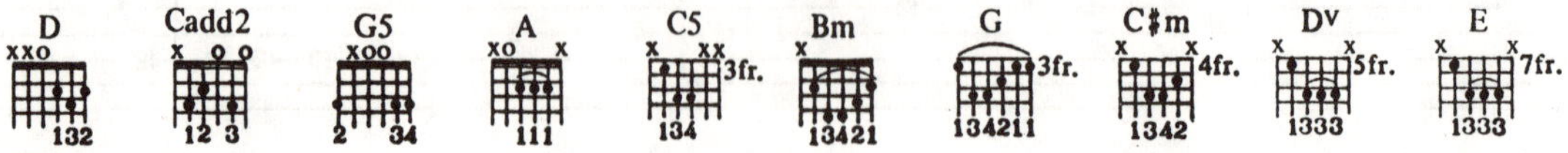

Tune down 1/2 step:
⑥=E♭ ③=G♭
⑤=A♭ ②=B♭
④=D♭ ①=E♭

Moderately slow Rock ♩ = 90

1st, 2nd, 3rd Verses
w/Rhy. Figs. 1 & 1A
3rd time w/Fill 1
D
3
C
G5
1. Yes - ter - day there was so man - y things I was nev - er told.
2.3. See additional lyrics
D
C
G5
Now that I'm start - in' to learn, I feel I'm grow - in' old. 'Cause
D
Cadd2
G5
Both gtrs.
yes - ter - day's got noth - in' for me. Old pic - tures that I'll al - ways see.
D
G5
1.
2.
pick slide
Time just fades the pag - es in my book of mem - o - ries. all just let them be
Rhy. Fig. 2 (*Gtr. I)
Chorus
A
⑤2fr.
B
C5
G5
Ooh, yes - ter - day's got noth - in' for me.
Riff A (*Gtr. II)
P P
P P
2 4 5 (5) 5 4 0 0 0 2 4
*w/distortion

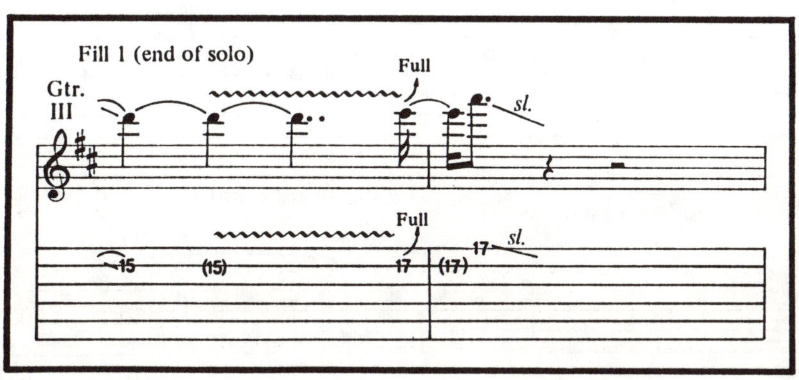
Fill 1 (end of solo)
Gtr. III
Full
sl.
Full
15 (15) 17 (17) 17
sl.

To Coda
A
⑤2fr.
B C5
Yes - ter - day's, ooh, got noth - in' for me.
G5
Guitar solo
Gtrs. I & II
Bm
G
Got noth - in' for me, yeah, ooh, yeah.
Gtr. III
Full
1/2
semi-harm.
sl.
Bm
G
C♯m
D
E
D.S. (take 2nd ending) al Coda
w/Rhy. Fig. 2 & Riff A (both last 2 bars only)
Coda G5
w/Rhy. Fig. 2 & Riff A
⑤ 2fr.
Yes - ter - day's got noth - in' for me.

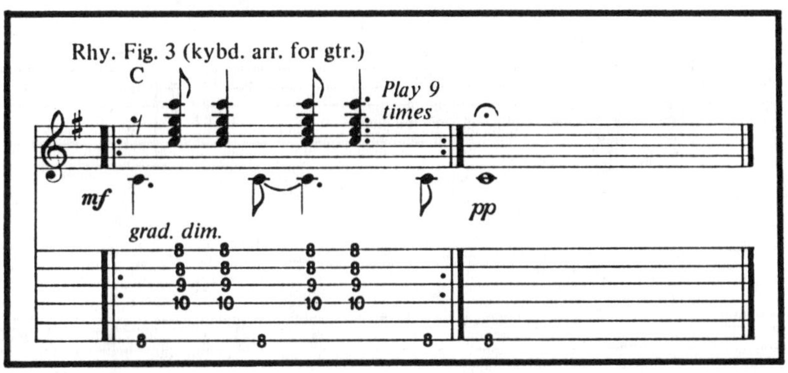

Additional Lyrics

2. Prayers in my pocket
And no hand in destiny.
I'll keep on movin' along
With no time to plant my feet.
'Cause yesterday's got nothin' for me.
Old pictures that I'll always see.
Some things could be better
If we'd all just let them be. *(To Chorus)*

3. Yesterday there were so many things
I was never shown.
Suddenly this time I found
I'm on the streets and I'm all alone.
Yesterday's got nothin' for me.
Old pictures that I'll always see.
I ain't got time to reminisce
Old novelties. *(To Chorus)*

KNOCKIN' ON HEAVEN'S DOOR

Words and Music by
Bob Dylan

*Vocal melody doubled one octave higher (till Chorus).

*During Chorus Gtr. I doubles Gtr. II w/slight rhythmic variations. Both gtrs. w/distortion.

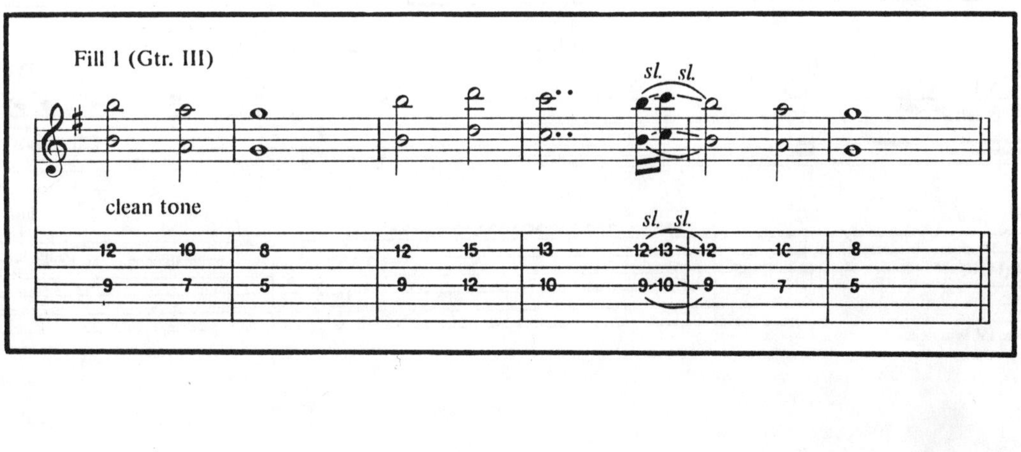

*Gtr. I w/clean tone; Gtr. IV is acous.

C G D C
yeah, yeah. Ow. (Whispered:) Choo, choo, choo.
8va
P Full Full 1/2 Full Full
sl.
G D C
2nd Verse
w/Fill 2
*w/sound effects
Gtr. V
Gtr. I
2. Ma-ma, put my guns in the ground.
(Ooh.
Full 1/2
*Sounds of ammunition shells ejected from guns.
Am
w/Fill 1
G5 D C
I can't shoot them an-y-more.
Ooh,
H
Fill 2 (Gtr. III)
(end of solo)

G5
D
Am
G5
D
That cold black cloud_ is com- in' down._
Ooh.)
Feels_ like I'm_ knock-in' on_ heav-en's door._
H
Chorus
Gtr. II
G5
Gtrs. I&II
G5
D5
C5
⑤3fr.
C
C5
P.M.
Knock, knock, knock-in' on_ heav-en's door,_ hey, hey,_ hey,_ hey,_
G5
D5
C5
G5
yeah. Knock, knock, knock - in' on_ heav-en's door.___
Gtr. III
w/distortion
sl.
D5
C5
⑤3fr.
C
C5
P.M.
Knock, knock, knock - in' on_ heav-en's door._ Ooh,_ yeah._
sl.

Guitar solo II
G5
D5
C5
*G5
Knock, knock, knock-in' on heav-en's door, hey, hey, yeah. Ooh.
*Gtr. I continues to double Gtr. II for 8 more bars.
let ring
both notes vib.
sl.
8va
Full
1/2
P
Dv
CIII
w/Rhy. Fill 1
C

Rhy. Fill 1 (Gtr. II)
let ring
sl.

Gtr. II
G5
loco
(Gtr. II out)
C5
D5
Gtr. I
Bb5
Fdbk:
(8va)
Fdbk.
(w/phone touch-tones and ringing)
(Gtr. III out)
(Spoken:) You just better start sniffin' your own rank subjugation, Jack, 'cause it's just you against your tattered libido, the bank and the mortician
forever, man, and it wouldn't be luck if you could get out of life

Chorus
G5 N.C.
N.C.(G5)
Bkgd. Voc. Fig. 1
alive. Knock, knock, knock-in' on heav-en's door, hey, hey, hey, hey, yeah.
(Knock, knock, knock-in' on heav-en's door.)
(Gtr. I out)
sl.
(C)
G5 D C
Knock, knock, knock- in' on heav-en's door. Ooh, yeah.
Gtr. II
pick w/fingers
w/Bkgd. Voc. Fig. 1
G5 D C
G5 D5
Knock, knock, knock-in' on heav-en's door.
Ooh, knock, knock, knock-in' on heav-en's door,
Gtr. I
clean tone w/chorus
Gtr. II
pick w/fingers
C5
w/Bkgd. Voc. Fig. 1
G5 D C
hmm, no, no, hmm, no, woh, woh.
Oh.
Gtr. I

G5
D
C
Knock, knock, knock - in' on heav-en's door,
no, no, hmm, no,
A.H.
(8va)
Gtr. II
sl.
pick w/fingers-
A.H.
sl.
A.H. pick: C♯
w/Bkgd. Voc. Fig. 1
G
N.C.
C5
no.
Door,
woh, woh, woh,
sl.
pick slide
sl.
P.M.
Chorus
w/Bkgd. Voc. Fig. 1 (4 times)
Gtr. II
G5
D5
C5
⑤3fr.
C
C5
P.M.
yeah.
Knock, knock, knock - in' on heav-en's door.
G5
D5
C5
⑤3fr.
C
C5
P.M.
Knock, knock, knock - in' on heav-en's door.
Ooh,
w/distortion
sl.

⑤3fr.
G5
D5
C5
C
C5
P.M.
yeah. Knock, knock, knock - in' on heav - en's door.
sl.
G5
D5
C5
Knock, knock, knock - in' on heav - en's door.
Uh, woh
Free time
w/Rhy. Fill 2
G5
woh, woh, oh, yeah, yeah. Ow!
Fdbk.
rit.
Fdbk. pitch: D
Rhy. Fill 2 (Gtr. II)
T
Fdbk.
(8va)
Fdbk. pitch: A

GET IN THE RING

Words and Music by
Slash, Duff McKagan
and W. Axl Rose

B♭5
F5
E♭5
Full
1/2
grad. bend
sl.
⑥3fr.
G
4fr.
A♭
5fr.
A
P
semi-
harm.
(end half time feel)
pick slide

Straight eigth feel
F5
Eb5
D5 Eb5 A Bb5
⑥5fr.
P.M.
Full
1/2
P
Rhy. Fig. 1 (Gtr. II)
(end Rhy. Fig. 1)
sl.
w/Rhy. Fig. 1
Rhy. Fig. 1A (Gtr. III)
(end Rhy. Fig. 1A)
D5 A Eb5
1st Verse
w/Rhy. Figs. 1 & 1A (both 3½ times)
Bb5
Why do you look at me when you hate me?
(Gtr. I out)
dim.
D5 A Bb5
Why should I look at you when you make me hate you too?
I sense a smell of ret - ri - bu - tion in the air.

D5 A B♭5
⑥5fr.
F5
E♭5
I don't e - ven un - der - stand why the fuck
you e - ven care.
Gtr. II
C5
Rhy. Fig. 2 (Gtr. II)
And I don't need
(I don't need
Rhy. Fill 1 (Gtr. III)
Rhy. Fig. 2A (Gtr. III)
P.M.
P.M.
F5VIII
C5
your jeal - ous - y, yeah.
your jeal - ous - y.)
P
let ring
sl.
Why drag me down in your mis - er - y.
(Why drag me down in your mis - er - y,
F5VIII

(end Rhy. Fig. 2)
Bb5
sl.
oh yeah.)
(end Rhy. Fig. 2A)
Rhy. Fig. 3
sl.
P.M.
⑤6fr.
Eb
Bb5
A.H.
(8va)
Full
Full
Full
2nd Verse
w/Rhy. Figs. 1 & 1A (both 3½ times)
F5
Eb5
⑥5fr.
D5 A Bb5
And when you stare you don't think I feel it,
Gtr. I
Fdbk.
(15ma)
but I'm gon-na deal it back to you in spades.
steady gliss.

⑥5fr.
F5
E♭5
D5 A B♭5
When I'm hav - in' fun, ya know I can't con-ceal it,
8va
sl.
F5
E♭5
w/Rhy. Fills 1 & 1A
'cause I know you'd nev - er cut it in my game, oh no.
(Gtr. I out)
steady gliss.
sl.
⑤open
D5 A C5
w/Rhy. Figs. 2 & 2A
F5VIII
And when you're talk - in' a - bout a vas - ec - to - my,
yeah,
C5
I'll be writ - in' down.
(I'll be writ - in' down.
Rhy. Fill 1A (Gtr. II)

F5VIII
Bb5
your o - bit - u - ar - y, his - to - ry,
your o - bit - u - ar - y, his - to - ry.)
w/Rhy. Fig. 3 (3 times)
Gtr. II
sl.
ow!
Rhy. Fig. 4 (Gtr. II)
Bridge
C5
Eb5
You got your bitch - es with the sil - i - cone in - jec - tions, crys - tal meth and yeast
Gtr. III
P.M.
Bb5I
C5
in - fec - tions, bleached blond hair, col - la - gen lip pro - jec - tions.
(end Rhy. Fig. 4)
w/Rhy. Fig. 4
Eb5
Who are you to crit - i - cize my in - ten - tions? Got your sub - tle, man - i - pu - la - tive de - vic - es.

B♭5
C5
Just like you, I got my vic - es.
I got a thought that would be nice, I'd like to
P.M.
sl.
Gtr. II
D♭5 C5 D♭5 C5
D5
crush your head tight in my vice.
Pain!!!
D
⑥8fr.
C B♭5

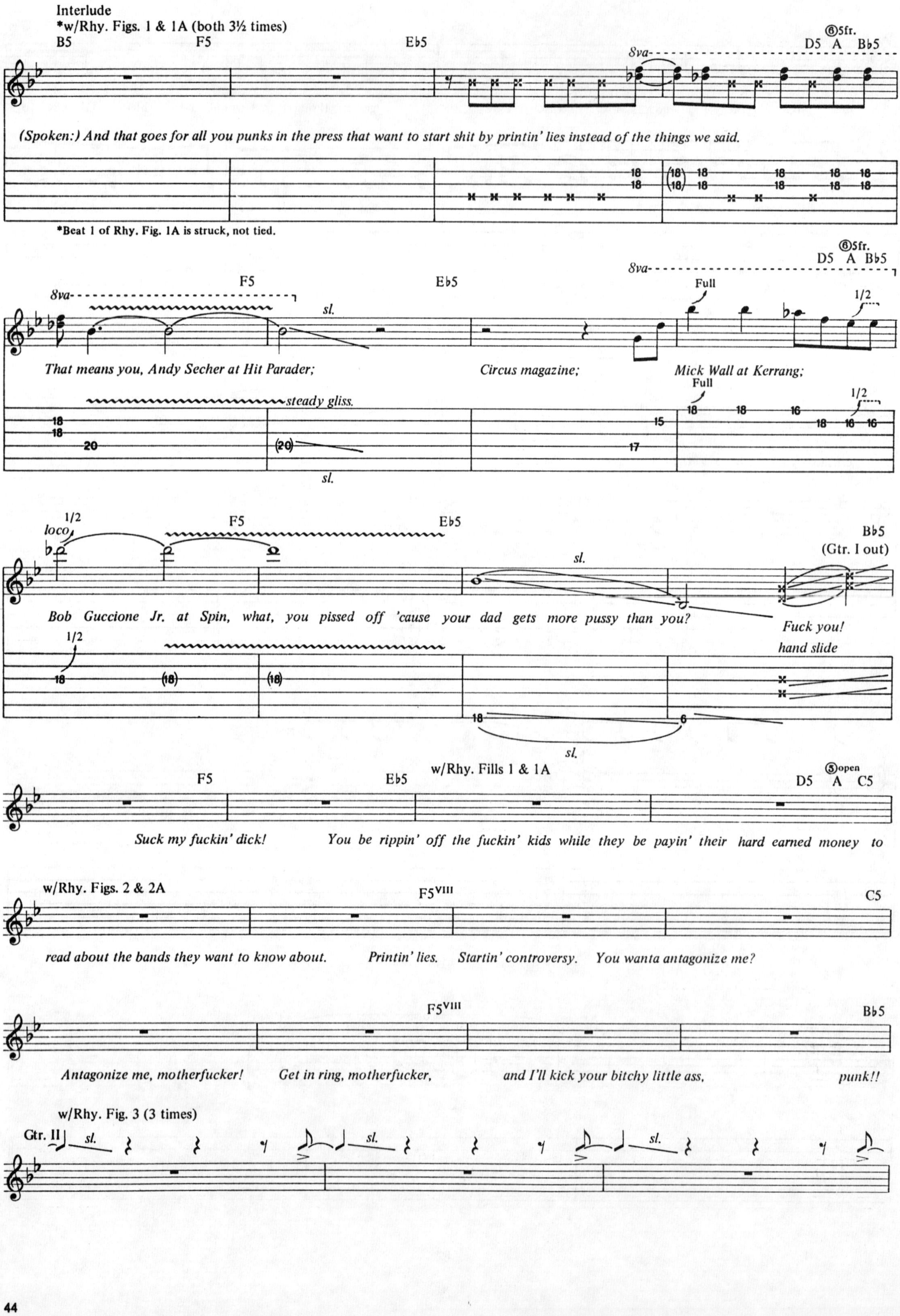
Interlude
*w/Rhy. Figs. 1 & 1A (both 3½ times)
B5 F5 Eb5 D5 A Bb5
(Spoken:) And that goes for all you punks in the press that want to start shit by printin' lies instead of the things we said.
*Beat 1 of Rhy. Fig. 1A is struck, not tied.
That means you, Andy Secher at Hit Parader;
Circus magazine;
Mick Wall at Kerrang;
steady gliss.
Bob Guccione Jr. at Spin, what, you pissed off 'cause your dad gets more pussy than you?
(Gtr. I out)
Fuck you!
hand slide
w/Rhy. Fills 1 & 1A
Suck my fuckin' dick!
You be rippin' off the fuckin' kids while they be payin' their hard earned money to
w/Rhy. Figs. 2 & 2A
read about the bands they want to know about.
Printin' lies.
Startin' controversy.
You wanta antagonize me?
Antagonize me, motherfucker!
Get in ring, motherfucker,
and I'll kick your bitchy little ass,
punk!!
w/Rhy. Fig. 3 (3 times)
Gtr. II

C5VIII
sl.
P.M.
Guitar solo I
D5
*Gtrs. II & III
(cont. in slashes)
*Gtr. III plays P.M. for next 8 bars.
Gtr. I
H
Full
1/2
P
8va
hold bend

D5
⑤3fr.
C
P.M.
I don't like you,
(Gtr. I out)
8va
dim.
(20)
D5
⑤3fr.
C
D5
P.M.
I just hate you. I'm gon
na kick your ass,
G5
E
oh yeah,
(Gtr. III cont. in notation)
A
D5
oh yeah
ow!
(w/laughter)
Gtr. II
Gtr. III
sl.
P.M.
H
C5

w/Rhy. Figs. 2 & 2A
F5VIII
You may not like our in - teg - ri - ty, yeah.
Gtr. III substitute Rhy. Fill 2
C5
Resume Rhy. Fig. 2A
F5VIII
We built a world out of an - ar - chy,
oh yeah!
Gtrs. II & III
Guitar solo II
Bb5
F5
w/Rhy. Figs. 1 & 1A (last 3 bars only)
Eb5
Gtr. I
Full
1/2
w/Rhy. Figs. 1 & 1A (both 7 times)
Bb5
F5
Rhy. Fill 2 (Gtr. III)
C5

(w/crowd cheering)
Eb5
Bb5
F5
(Spoken:) And in this corner,
weighing in at 850 pounds,
Guns N' Roses.
Full
sl.
P
8va-
loco
1/2
H
Get in the ring.
Get in the ring.
Get in the ring.
Get in the ring.

F5
Eb5
Voc. Fig. 1
Get in the ring.
(Moth - er fuck - er.)
Get in the ring.
Get in the ring.
1/2
Full
*w/Voc. Fig. 1 (9 times)
Bb5
F5
Eb5
*w/crowd chanting "Get in the ring" till end.
Free time
Gtrs. II & III
sl.
(Band out)
Yeah!
(Spoken:) This song is dedicated to all the Guns N' fuckin' Roses fans who stuck with us through all the fucking shit. And to all
those opposed...hmm...well?

SHOTGUN BLUES

Words and Music by
W. Axl Rose

C5 F/C C5 A5 D/A A5
Fuck, they move it ev - e - ry time.
You walk a mile in my shoes,
B5 E/B B5
and then you tell me 'bout sing - in' the blues.
Pre-chorus
(Gtrs. I&II) B5
Ah, well, you get what you pay for.
A5 G♯5 A5 G♯5 A5 B5 A♯5 B5 A♯5 B5 A5
An free - dom's real high - priced.
An while you're rip - pin' off chil - dren,
G♯5 A5 G♯5 A5 *D5 C♯5 D5 C♯5 D5 E5
some - bod - y's fuck - in' your wife.
Ooh, it's nev - er made a dif - f'rence.
*Gtr. I substitute D5^V, C♯5^IV, E5^VII and D♯5^VI (next 4 bars).
1. D♯5 E5 D♯5 E5
2. D♯5 E5 D♯5 E5
It's on - ly how you sur - vive.
I got the mak - in' a stance. An I'm
Bridge
F♯5^XIV C♯5 B5 C♯5 D5 C♯5 D5 E5
Gtr. II
tired of the frus - tra - tion of liv - in' in - side of your lies.
Gtr. I
D♯5 E5 F♯5^XIV C♯5 B5 C♯5 D5
And I'm wired on in - dig - na - tion. I said
sl.

C♯5 D5 E5
sl.
some - bod - y's got to die.
w/Fill 1
Guitar solo
Gtrs. I & II
F♯5
E5II F♯5
Gtr. III
sl.
E5II F♯5 A5
D5V
F♯5
Oh,
Full
H P
P H
Fill 1
Gtr. III
sl.
steady gliss.
19

E5II F#5 E5II A5
yeah.
Fuck.
G#5 A5 G#5 F#5 E5II F#5 E5II F#5 A5
D5V F#5 E5II F#5
E5II F#5 E5II B5
Ooh.
Ah.

w/Rhy. Fig. 1
E5 A/E E5 C♯5 F♯/C♯ C♯5 D5 G D5
Ah.
(Come on.)
Full 2
(Gtr. III out)
sl.
steady gliss.
12 (12) (12) (12) 13 12 (12) (12)
E5 A/E E5 C♯5 F♯/C♯ C♯5 D5 G/D D5
I got the
Chorus
w/Rhy. Fig. 1 (2 times)
E5 A/E E5 C♯5 F♯/C♯ C♯5 D5 G
shot - gun blues, shot - gun blues. I said I don't know what I did, but I
D5 E5 A/E E5 C♯5 F♯/C♯ C♯5 D5
know I got - ta move. I got the shot - gun blues, shot - gun blues. I
G/D D5 E5 A/E E5 C♯5
can't wait here for - ev - er. I got too much here to lose. I got the shot - gun blues, shot -
F♯/C♯ C♯5 D5 G D5
gun blues. Well, lis - ten, moth - er, fuck - er, you're a - bout to pay your dues. I got the
E5 A/E E5 C♯5 F♯/C♯ C♯5 D5 G/D
shot - gun blues, shot - gun blues. If you're go - in' up a - gainst me, then you
D5 Rhy. Fig. 3 (Gtrs. I & II) G/D D5 (end Rhy. Fig. 3)
know you're gon - na lose. Ooh, I (I
w/Rhy. Fig. 3 (6 times)
G/D D5 G/D D5
know.
know there's ways that

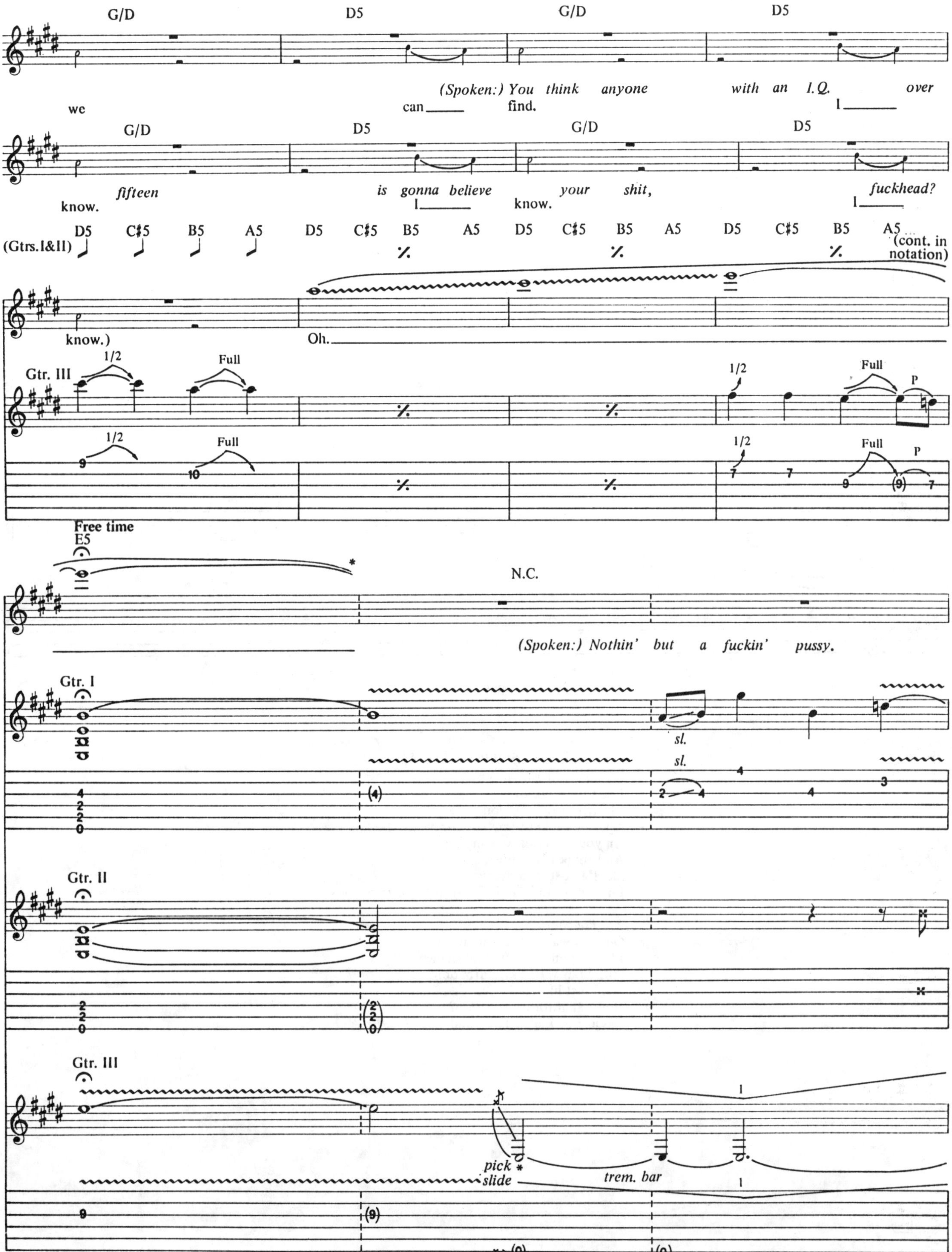

*Continue ad lib (next 3 bars).

*Pick slide causes open stg. to sound.

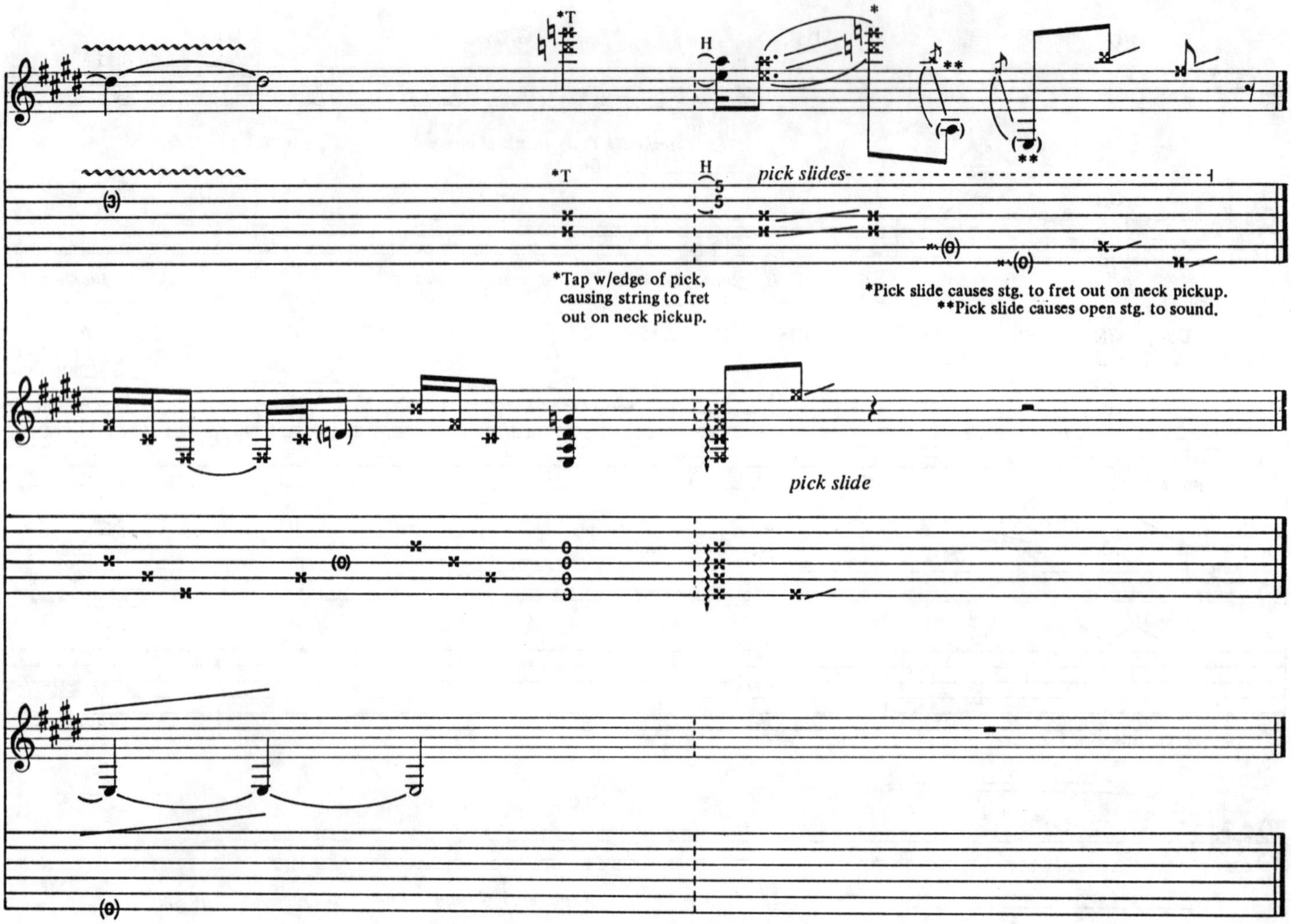

Additional Lyrics

2. An now you ask me why.
I said it's do or die.
I'll stick it right in your face.
And then I'll put you in your motherfuckin' place.
An you, you can suck my ass.
An I think it's so low-class.
Me, I'm just so concerned.
I'm still waitin' for your ass to burn.

2nd Pre-chorus:
Oh, you want a confrontation.
I'll give you every fuckin' chance
With your verbal masturbation.
Me, I just like to dance.
How's that for provocation?
I'm just makin' a stance and I'm... *(To Bridge)*

BREAKDOWN

Words and Music by
W. Axl Rose

A
D
H
sl.
Full
1/2
(Gtr. I out)
H P
(Gtr. II out)
Rhy. Fig. 1
G/B
We all come in from the cold. We
Csus2
come down from the wi - re. An ev-'ry-bod-y warms them-selves to a dif-f'rent
Dsus4 D Dsus2 D G/B Csus2
fi - re. When some-times we get burned, you'd think some-time we'd learn. The
Gtr. IV
Fdbk.
(8va)
P
vol. off
w/dist.
mf
Fdbk. pitch: A

G/B
A
one you love is the one that should take you high - er.
You ain't
sl.
1/2
P
(end Rhy. Fig. 1) w/Rhy. Fig. 1
G
D/F♯
A/E
D
G/B Csus2
G/B
got no one. You bet - ter go back out and find her.
Full
Rhy. Fig. 2
A
D
Dsus4 D Dsus2 D
G/B Csus2
G/B
Gtr. V
w/dist.
(Gtr. IV)
(end Rhy. Fig. 2)

A
G
D/F♯
A/E
(Gtr. D
III)
(Gtr. V out)
(Gtr. IV out)
G
D
G
Gtr. II
mf let ring
sl.
Double time 𝅗𝅥 = 164
D
1. Just like chil - dren hid - in' in a clos - et can't tell what's
(Gtr. II out) 2. See additional lyrics
(Gtr. IV)
Gtr.IV
f
A
⑥2fr. 3fr.
F♯ G
G
go - in' on out - side, some - times we're so far off the beat -

D
en track, we'll get a - tak - en for a ride by a
H
H
Rhy. Fig. 3A
G A D/F♯ G
par - lor trick or some words of wit, a hid - den hand up a sleeve.
Rhy. Fig. 3
To think that the one you love could hurt you now is a
A
lit - tle hard to be - lieve. But

D
ev - 'ry - bod - y, dar - lin', some - times bites the hand_ that feeds._
1.
Half time feel
G
(end half time feel)
(end Rhy. Fig. 3A)
D
D6
D
D6
Ow!
(end Rhy. Fig. 3)
2.
Half time feel
G
Ooh,_ yeah, yeah,_ ow!_ Break -

Chorus
D
G
down!
Let me hear it now.
Break - down!
Rhy. Fig. 4
D
Let me hear it now.
Yeah.
(end Rhy. Fig. 4)
w/Rhy. Fig. 4
G
Break - down!
Let me hear it now.
A
(end half time feel)
Ow!
Get down with yo' bad self!
Al - right!
(Gtr. IV)

Guitar solo
w/Rhy. Fig. 5 (2 times)
D
Rhy. Fig. 5A
Gtr. VI
Full
1/2
Csus2
G/B
3/4
P
A
1½
8va
(end Rhy. Fig. 5A)
w/Rhy. Fig. 5A
D
H
loco
grad. bend
hold bend
sl.
Rhy. Fig. 5
D5
Gtr. IV

Tempo I
(Gtr. III)
G
D/F♯
A/E
H
1/2
w/Rhy. Fig. 2 (Gtr. V)
D
Csus2
G/B
(Gtr. VI out)
sl.
(Gtr. IV)
A
D
Csus2
G/B
w/Rhy. Fill 1
A
H H
G
D/F♯
A/E
D
*Csus2
I've come to know the cold. I think of it as home. When there ain't e -
*Chord names in next 3 bars refer to piano and bass.
Rhy. Fill 1
A5
Gtr. V
G5
D/F♯
N.C.
D
(Gtr. V out)

G/B
A
nough of me_ to go a - round,_ I'd rath - er be left a - lone._ But if I
Full
vol. off
mf
14
w/Rhy. Fig. 2 (1st 4 bars only) (Gtr. V)
D
(Gtr. III)
Csus2
call you out_ of hab - it, I'm out of love and I got - ta have_ it. Would you
P
15
17
(17)
G/B
A
give it to me_ if I fit your needs,_ like when we both knew_ we had it? But
8va
grad. bend
Double time ♩= 164
w/Rhy. Figs. 3 & 3A
G
A
D/F♯
G
now the dam - age's done,_ and we're back out on_ the run._ Fun - ny how

A
ev - 'ry - thing was ros - es when we held on to the guns.
Just be - cause you're win - nin' don't mean you're the luck - y ones.
D
3
Half time feel
G
(Ooh,
ooh.)
w/Rhy. Fig. 4
Chorus
D
(Gtr.III)
Break - down!
Let me hear it now.
G
Break - down!
Yeah.
Asus4
(Gtr. IV)
A
D
D7
G7
Break - down!
Break - down.
P
P.M.

Let me hear it now.
Asus4
A
(end half-time feel)
1/4
1/2
H
P
Outro
Rhy. Fig. 6A
Csus2
D
(end Rhy. Fig. 6A)
(Gtr. VI)
Full
Rhy. Fig. 6 (Gtr. IV)
(end Rhy. Fig. 6)
w/Rhy. Figs. 6 & 6A (both 9 times)
Csus2
D

Csus2
D
(Spoken:) There goes the challenger,
being chased by the blue, blue meanies on wheels. The vicious traffic squad
cars are after our lone driver, the last American hero,
the, the Electric Sintar, the demi-god, the super driver of the
Golden West! Two nasty Nazi cars are close behind
the beautiful, lone driver. The police cars are getting closer, closer,
8va-
loco
Full
1/4
1/2
sl.
P
H
rake

D
Full Full
P
closer to our soul hero in his soul mobile.
Csus2
Full
D
1/2
Yeah, baby! They about to strike. They gonna get him. Smash! Rape!
grad. bend
Csus2
The last beautiful free soul on this planet.
sl.
(Gtr. III)
(cont. in notation)
(Gtr. IV)
(cont. in slashes)

Additional Lyrics

2. When I look around, everybody always brings me down.
Well, is it them or me? Well, I just can't see. But there ain't no peace to be found.
But if someone really cared, well, they'd take the time to spare
A moment to try and understand another one's despair.
Remember, in this game we call life that no one said it's fair.

PRETTY TIED UP
(THE PERILS OF ROCK N' ROLL DECADENCE)

Words and Music by
Izzy Stradlin'

D5
Gtr. III
Gtr. I
Rhy. Fig. 3
w/Fill 1 (Gtr. III)
sl.
w/Rhy. Figs. 1, 1A & 2
Play 4 times
1st, 2nd, 3rd Verses
w/Rhy. Figs. 1, 1A & 2 (all 4 times)
1. I know this chick, she lives down on Mel - rose.
2.3. See additional lyrics
She ain't sat - is - fied with - out some pain.
(Oo.)
G5
B5
D
4 open
Fri - day night is go - in' up in - side her... a - gain.
Well,
crack the whip 'cause that bitch is just in - sane. (Spoken:) I'm serious.
Oh, she's pret - ty tied
G5
F♯5
E5
D5
pick slide
A
C
* Chorus melody doubled an octave higher.
Fill 1
Harm.
(8va)
H

Chorus
Rhy. Fig. 4
Gtr. III
D5
C5
G5
A5
C5
(end Rhy. Fig. 4)
w/Rhy. Figs. 4 & 4A
up hang-in' up-side down. She's pret-ty tied up an you can ride her. She's pret-ty tied
Rhy. Fig. 4A
Gtr. I
1/2
sl.
To Coda
1.
(end Rhy. Fig. 5)
Rhy. Fig. 5
⑥open
E
Rhy. Fig.
F5
up hang-in' up-side down. Ooh. I can't tell
Rhy. Fig. 6A
(end Rhy. Fig. 6)
w/Fill 1
you she's the right one. Oh no, oh no, oh no.
2.
w/Rhy. Figs. 6 & 6A
Oh, but I can't tell

Guitar solo I
D5
Gtrs. I & III
C5
you she's the right one. Oh no, oh no, oh no.
Gtr. IV
w/wah
Full
P
H
B5
1/2
Rhy. Fig. 7
(Gtrs. I & III)
(end Rhy. Fig. 7)
8va
grad. bend
sl.
w/Rhy. Fig. 7 (2 times)

w/Fill 2 (Gtr. V)
D5
F5
G5
Gtrs. I&III
Gtr. III
loco
w/Rhy. Fig. 3
Full
D.S. al Coda
grad. bend
w/Rhy. Fig. 4 (2 times Gtr. III)
G5
E F5
G5
A5 C5 D5
C5 G5
(Gtr. III)
Coda
(Gtrs. I&III)
Rhy. Fig. 8 Gtr. I
I can't tell you she's the right one.
(cont. in slashes)
Gtr. IV
Fill 2
Harm.

(end Rhy. Fig. 8)
A5
C5
w/Rhy. Fig. 8
D5
C5
G5
w/Vocal ad lib. (till end)
A5
C5
She's the right one.
w/Rhy. Fig. 5 (Gtr. III)
D5
Gtr. I
C5
G5
w/Rhy. Fig. 6
F5
G5
Rhy. Fig. 9 Gtr. III
w/Rhy. Fig. 7 (till end - Gtr. I)
D5
(C5)
(end Rhy. Fig. 9)
w/Rhy. Fig. 9 (2 times)
D5
C5
D5

C5
D5
C5
w/Rhy. Fig. 9 (3 times)
D5
C5
D5
C5
D5
C5
D5
grad. bend
w/Rhy. Fig. 10 (Gtr. V - till end)
C5
D5
C5
Rhy. Fig. 10

Additional Lyrics

2. Once there was this rock n' roll band rollin' on the streets.
   Time went by and it became a joke.
   We just needed more and more fulfilling–uh-huh.
   Time went by and it all went up in smoke.
   But check it out. *(To Chorus)*

3. Once you made that money, it costs more now.
   It might cost a lot more than you'd think.
   I just found a million dollars that someone forgot.
   It's days like this that push me o'er the brinks.
   *Cool and stressing. *(To Chorus)*

**Pronounced "Kool Ranch Dres'ing"*

LOCOMOTIVE
(COMPLICITY)

Words and Music by
Slash and W. Axl Rose

Rhy. Fig. 1 (Gtr. I)
G5
F♯5
E5
Rhy. Fig. 1A (Gtr. II)
(end Rhy. Fig. 1)
(end Rhy. Fig. 1A)
A5
Gtr. II
Gtr. I
Rhy. Fig. 2
A5II
(end Rhy. Fig. 2)
P.M.
w/Rhy. Fig. 2 (Gtr. I)
N.C.(A5)
Full

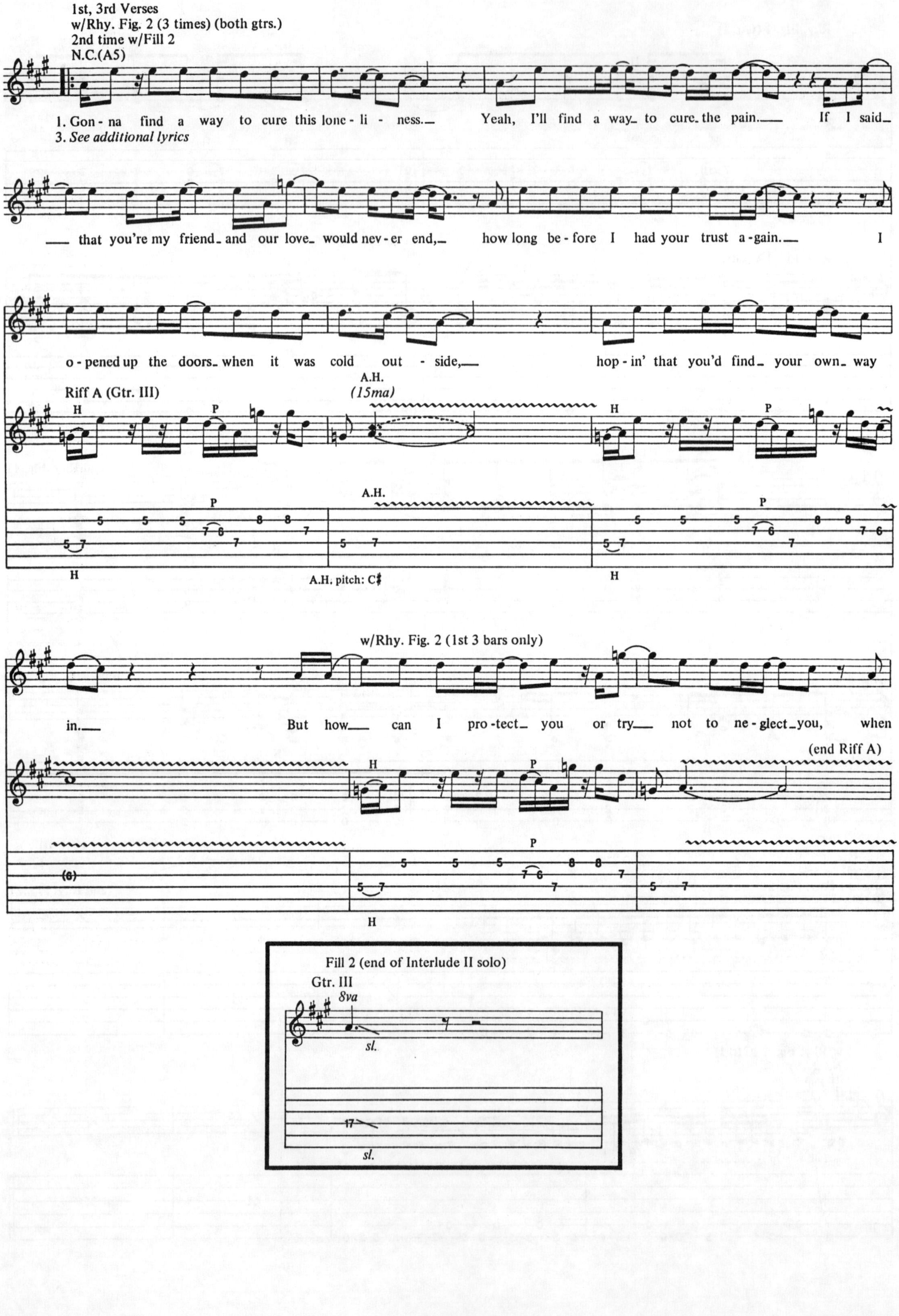
1st, 3rd Verses
w/Rhy. Fig. 2 (3 times) (both gtrs.)
2nd time w/Fill 2
N.C.(A5)
1. Gon - na find a way to cure this lone - li - ness. Yeah, I'll find a way to cure the pain. If I said
3. See additional lyrics
that you're my friend and our love would nev - er end, how long be - fore I had your trust a - gain. I
o - pened up the doors when it was cold out - side, hop - in' that you'd find your own way
Riff A (Gtr. III)
A.H.
(15ma)
H
P
A.H. pitch: C♯
w/Rhy. Fig. 2 (1st 3 bars only)
in. But how can I pro - tect you or try not to ne - glect you, when
(end Riff A)
Fill 2 (end of Interlude II solo)
Gtr. III
8va
sl.

w/Rhy. Fill 1
F♯5
Gtrs. I & II
A5
you won't take the love I have to give?
I bought me an il-lu-sion an I
Play next 6 bars 2nd time only
H
P
sl.
put it on the wall.
F♯5
A5
I let it fill my head with dreams and I had
to have them all.
F♯5
G5 F♯5 E5
w/Rhy. Figs. 1 & 1A
But oh, the taste is nev-er so sweet as what you be-lieve it is, well I guess
(Gtr. III out)

Rhy. Fill 1
(Gtrs. I & II)
N.C.(A5)
F♯5
P.M.

G5 F♯5 E5
G5
— it nev - er is.— It's these prej - u - diced- il - lu - sions that pump the blood- to the heart of the biz.—
Interludes I & III
w/Rhy. Fig. 2 (Gtrs. I & II)
N.C.(A5)
Play 1st time only
Gtr. III
Play 2nd time only
Gtr. III
Full
1/2
2. You

2nd, 4th Verses
w/Rhy. Fig. 2 (3 times)
N.C.(A5)
know I nev - er thought that it could take so long.
You know I nev - er knew how to be strong.
(Gtr. III out)
sl.
(Gtr. III out)
sl.
Yeah, I let you shape me but I feel as though you raped me, 'cause you climbed
in - side my world and in my songs.
w/Riff A
So now I've closed the door to keep the
Play 2nd time only (Gtr. IV)
H
P
cold out - side.
Seems some - how I've found the will to live.
But

w/Rhy. Fig. 2 (1st 3 bars only)
w/Fill 1 (both times)
how can I for-get_ you, or try___ not to re-ject_ you, when we both know it takes_ time to for-give,___
N.C.(D5)
G5
yeah.___
(Gtr. IV out)
Gtrs. I & II
Fill 1 (Gtr. III)

Pre-chorus
Rhy. Fig. 3
(Gtr. II)
A5 G♯5 G5(type 2) F♯5(type 2) F5 E5VII E♭5 D5 C5 A C5
(end Rhy. Fig. 3)
1. Sweet - ness is a vir - tue, and you lost your vir - tue long a - go. You
2.3. See additional lyrics
Rhy. Fig. 3A (Gtr. I)
(end Rhy. Fig. 3A)
*Lead vocal is tripled (sung one octave higher and one octave lower) throughout Pre-chorus and Chorus.
w/Rhy. Figs. 3 & 3A (2 times)
know I'd like to hurt you, but my con - science al - ways tells me no. You could
sell your bod - y on the street to an - y - one whom you might meet who'd
Gtr. II
A5 G♯5 G5(type 2) F♯5(type 2) F5 E5(type 2) C5
Chorus
A5 E G A G
love to try and get in - side. and bust your in - no - cence o - pen wide, 'cause my ba-by's got a lo - co - mo - tive. My
Gtr. I
sl.
ba-by's gone off the track. My ba-by's got a lo - co - mo - tive, got ta peel the bitch off my back.

3rd time to Coda
D5 A5 D5 A5 N.C. D5 A5 D5 A5 N.C. D5 A5 D5 A5 N.C.
I know it looks like I'm in - sane.
Take a clos - er look I'm
Gtrs. I & II
Rhy. Fig. 4
1.
D5 A5 C5
not to blame, no.
Interlude II
w/Rhy. Fig. 1 (Gtr. I & II)
N.C.(A5)
Rhy. Fill 2
Gtr. III
sl.
8va
2.
w/Rhy. Fill 2
D5 A5 C5
not to blame, no.
(cont. in Fill 2)
Full
Gtr. III
fade in

Guitar solo
w/Rhy. Fig. 2 (1st 3 bars only) (Gtr. II)
N.C.(A5)
Full
1/2
P
Gtr. I
P.M.
w/Rhy. Fill 3
N.C.(D5)
H P
Gtr. I & II
Rhy. Fill 3 (Gtr. II)

N.C.(A5)
N.C.(B5)
Full
1/2
H
P.M.
(Gtr. II cont. in slashes)
Gtr. II
⑥ 7fr.
5fr.
B
A
G5
F♯5
E5
Gtr. I
sl.
semi harm.
A5
(Gtr. II cont. in notation)
F5
E♭5
D5
C5
D.S. al Coda
don't pick
Gtrs. I & II

Coda
w/Rhy. Fig. 4 (both gtrs.)
D5 A5 D5 A5 N.C.
w/Rhy. Fig. 4 (3 times) (Gtr. II)
not to blame.
Yeah.
Gtr. I
w/1st bar of Rhy. Fill 2 (Gtr. II)
C5
Gtr. II
If love is blind I guess I'll buy my-self a cane.
*Gtrs. I & II sustain for 3 bars.
Outro
Am
G5 F5
*Gtr. V
clean tone
*Piano arr. for gtr.
Gtr. VI
w/wah
trem. bar
slight vib. w/bar
vib. w/bar
G F

Am
F
trem. bar
slight vib. w/bar
Rhy. Fig. 5
(end Rhy. Fig. 5)
w/Rhy. Fig. 5 (till end)
Am
Full
vib. w/bar
F
vib. w/bar
trem. bar
1/2
Am
Voc. Fig. 1
F
(end Voc. Fig. 1)
Love's
so
strange.
sl.
vib. w/bar
w/Voc. Fig. 1 (till end)
Am
F
sl.

Am
sl.
F
1/2
Am
P
H
F
Am
Full
F
Am
Full
F
Full

Am
F
Am
F
Am
F
Am
8va
loco
sl.
H
P
Full
1/2

Additional Lyrics

3. Gonna have some with my frustration.
Gonna watch the big screen in my head.
I'd rather take a detour 'cause this road ain't gettin' clearer.
Your train of thought has cut me off again.
Better tame that boy 'cause he's a wild one,
Better tame that boy for he's a man.
Sweetheart, don't make me laugh, you's gettin' too big for your pants,
And I's think maybe you should cut out while you can.
You can use your illusion, let it take you where it may.
We live and learn, and then sometimes it's best to walk away.
Me, I'm just here hangin' on,
It's my only place to stay, at least for now anyway.
I've worked too hard for my illusions just to throw them all away. *(To Interlude III)*

4. I'm taking time for quiet consolation,
In passing by this love that's passed away.
I know it's never easy, so why should you believe me
When I've always got so many things to say?
Calling off the dogs, a simple choice is made,
'Cause playful hearts can sometimes be enraged.
You know I tried to wake you, I mean how long could it take you
To open up your eyes and turn the page.

2nd Pre-chorus:
Kindness is a treasure and it's one towards me you've seldom shown.
So I'll say it for good measure, to all the one's like you I've known.
Ya know I'd like to shave your head and all my friends could paint it red.
'Cause love to me's a two way street an all I really want is peace. *(To Chorus)*

3rd Pre-chorus:
Affection is a blessing, can you find it in your sordid heart?
I tried to keep this thing ta-gether, but the tremor tore my pad apart.
Yeah, I know it's hard to face when all we've worked for's gone to waste.
But you're such a stupid woman and I'm such a stupid man, but love like time's got it's own plans. *(To Chorus)*

SO FINE

(Dedicated To Johnny Thunders)

Words and Music by
Duff McKagan

Bmadd4 C G Gmaj7 Bmadd4 C D
Uh.
(Draw breath)
Ah.
(end Rhy. Fig. 1A)
sl.
1st, 2nd Verses
w/Rhy. Fig. 1A (2 times)
G Gmaj7 Bmadd4 C G Gmaj7
1. How could she look so fine?
2. How could she be so cool?
Ah.
How could it be she might
How could she be so fine?
Rhy. Fig. 1B
Gtr. I
(end Rhy. Fig. 1B)
Bmadd4 C D G Gmaj7 Bmadd4 C
be mine?
How could she be so cool?
I owe a fa - vor to a friend.

G
Gmaj7
Bmadd4
C
D
I've been tak-en for a fool so man-y times.
My friends, they al-ways come through for me, yeah.
Hey.
*Play cue notes 2nd time.
w/Rhy. Fig. 2 (2 times)
Em
Am
C
It's (a) sto-ry of a man (who) works (as) hard as (he) can just to be a man who stands on his own
Gtr. II
*Play cue notes 2nd time.
Em
Am
1.
C
But the book al-ways burns as the sto-ry takes its turn an leaves a bro-ken man.
Rhy. Fig. 2
Gtr. I

2.
w/Rhy. Fig. 2 (2 times)
C
Em
Am
sto - ry takes its turn an leaves a bro - ken man.
If you could on - ly live my life,
H
C
E
Am
C
you could see the dif - f'rence you make to me, to me.
I'd
(Gtr. II out)
Double time ♩ = 140
2nd time w/Fill 1
D5 D6 D5 D6 E5
G5 G6 G5 G6 D5 D6 D5
look right up at night,
and all I'd see was dark - ness.
Now I
Rhy. Fig. 3
Gtr. III
(end Rhy. Fig. 3)
f w/dist.
P.M.
sl.
Fill 1
Gtr. IV
dim.

w/Rhy. Fig. 3(2½ times)
D6 D5 D6 E5
G5 G6 G5 G6 D5 D6 D5
see the stars al - right.
I wan - na reach right up and grab one for you. When the
D6 D5 D6 E5
G5 G6 G5 G6 D5 D6 D5
lights went down in your house,
yeah, that made me hap - py. The
To Coda
D5 D6 D5 D6 E5
Gtr. III G5
sweat I make for you,
yeah, I think you know where that comes from. Gui - tar, come on.
Gtr. IV
w/slide
Tempo I
Guitar solo
w/Rhy. Figs. 1 & 1A (both 2 times)
(Gtr. III out)
Bmadd4 C G Gmaj7 Bmadd4 C D
G Gmaj7 Bmadd4 C G Gmaj7
Gtr. III
⑥15fr.
D.S. al Coda
G
sl.
Yeah! Well, I'd
(cont. in Fill 1)

Coda
Gtr. III
G5
(Gtr. III out)
Tempo I
3rd Verse
w/Rhy. Figs. 1A (1¾ times) & 1B
G
Gmaj7
I think you know where that comes from.
3. How could she look so good?
Bmadd4
C
G
Gmaj7
w/Rhy. Fill 1
Bmadd4
C
D
(Whispered:) So good.
How could she be so fine?
w/Rhy. Fig. 1B
G
Gmaj7
Bmadd4
C
G
Gmaj7
(Draw breath) How could she be so cool?
Oh.
How could it be she might
Bmadd4
C
N.C.
Free time
G
be mine?
Ah.
Yeah.
Gtr. I
rit.
Gtr. II
rit.
Rhy. Fill 1
Gtr. I

ESTRANGED

Words and Music by
W. Axl Rose

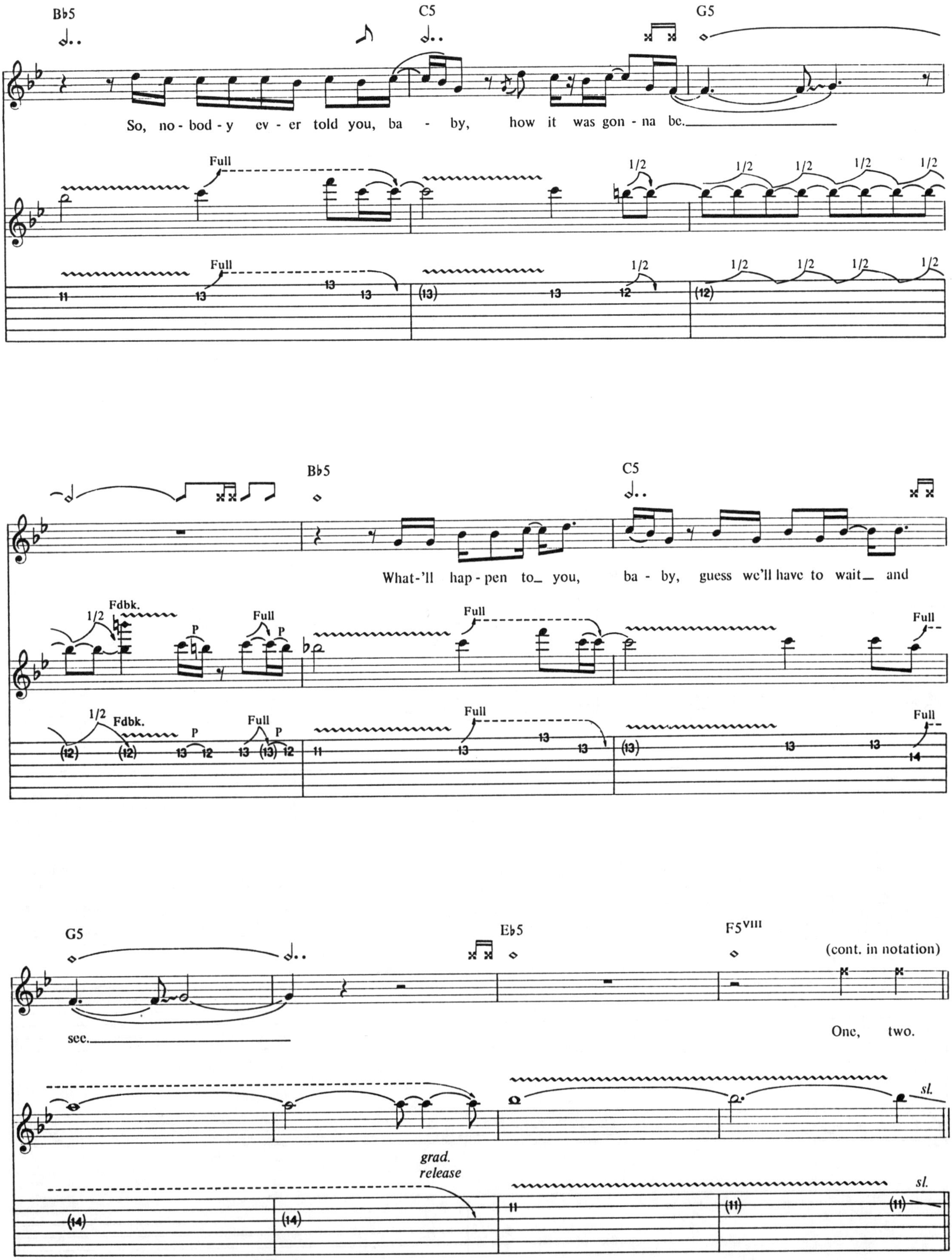
B♭5
C5
G5
So, no-bod-y ev-er told you, ba-by, how it was gon-na be.
Full
1/2
What-'ll hap-pen to you, ba-by, guess we'll have to wait and
Fdbk.
P
see.
E♭5
F5VIII
(cont. in notation)
One, two.
grad. release
sl.

G5
Riff A
Gtr. II
C5
Eb5
F5
Gtr. I
mf
Full
(end Riff A)
sl.
P

Gm
F
Eb
N.C.
Gm
Old at heart, but I'm on - ly twen - ty - eight. And I'm much too young to let love break my heart.
Fdbk.
(8va)
Fdbk.
Fdbk. pitch: D
(Gtr. I out)
F
Eb
N.C.
Young at heart, but it's get - ting much too late to find our - selves so far a -
8va
1/2
sl.
loco
p sl.
Gtr. I
G5
F5
G5
part. I don't know how you're s'posed to find me late - ly.
Full
Fdbk.
(Gtr. II out)
grad. bend
F5
G5
F5
And what more could you ask from me? How could you say that I nev - er need -

w/Fill 1
G5 Eb5 D5 F5VII
(cont. in notation)
ed you_ when you took ev - 'ry - thing,_ said you took ev - 'ry - thing_ from me?_
w/Riff A
G5 C5 Eb5 F5 G5 C5 Eb5 F5
Yi._
Gtr. I
G5 Eb5 F5 G5 Eb5 F5
Fdbk.
(8va)
*Let fdbk. sustain through next 2 bars.
Gm F Eb N.C. Gm
Young at heart, an it gets so hard to wait_ when no one I know can seem to help_ me now._
Gtr. II
Fdbk.
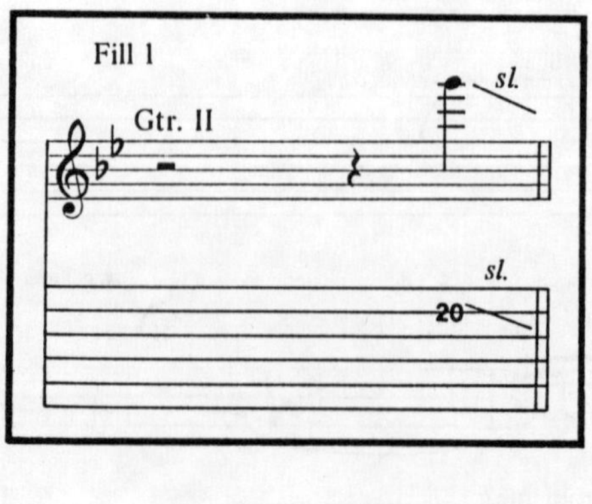
Fill 1
Gtr. II
sl.

F
Eb
N.C.
Gm
Old at heart, but I mustn't hes - i - tate_ if I'm to find_ my own way out._____ Still
8va
sl.
Gm7
C
talk - in' to my - self and no - bod - y's home. (Whispered:) A - lone._
Gtr. I
vol. off
mp
f
(cont. in slashes)
*8va applies to Gtr. II only.
G5
C5
Full
P
Bb5
So, no - bod - y ev - er told us, ba - by, how it was gon - na be._
1/2
A.H.
(8va)

Bb5
C5
So, what-'ll hap-pen to_ us, ba - by, guess we'll have to wait_ and
Full
Full
P
G5
C5
dim.
(Gtr. I out)
sce.
(Gtr. II out)
N.C.(C5)
(Bass gtr. & piano)
(Eb5)
(C5)
(Eb5)
w/Fill 2
C5
Gtr. III
Eb5
mf
Fill 2
Gtr. IV
mp
clean tone

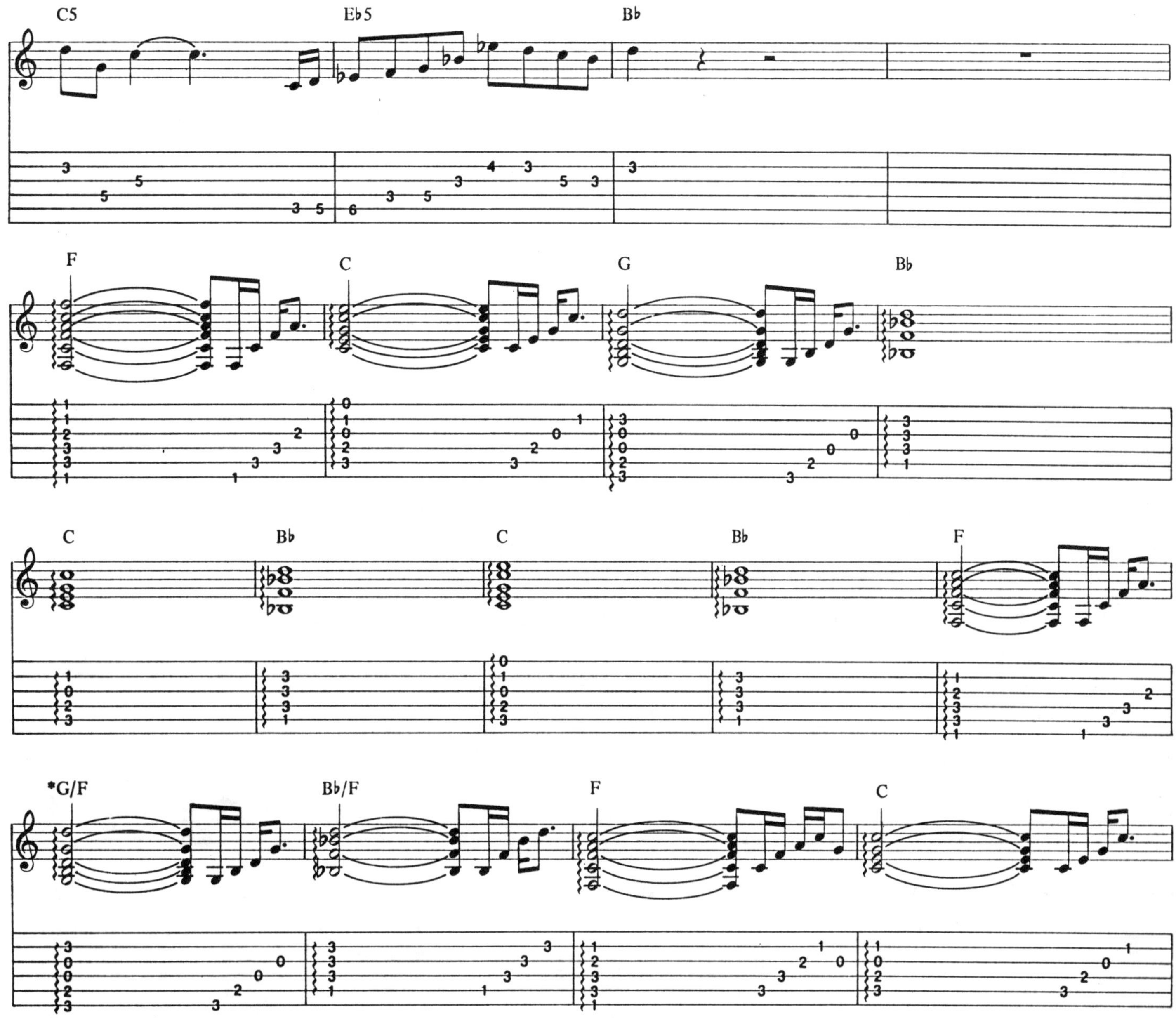

*Bass in chord names refers to bass gtr. (next 2 bars).

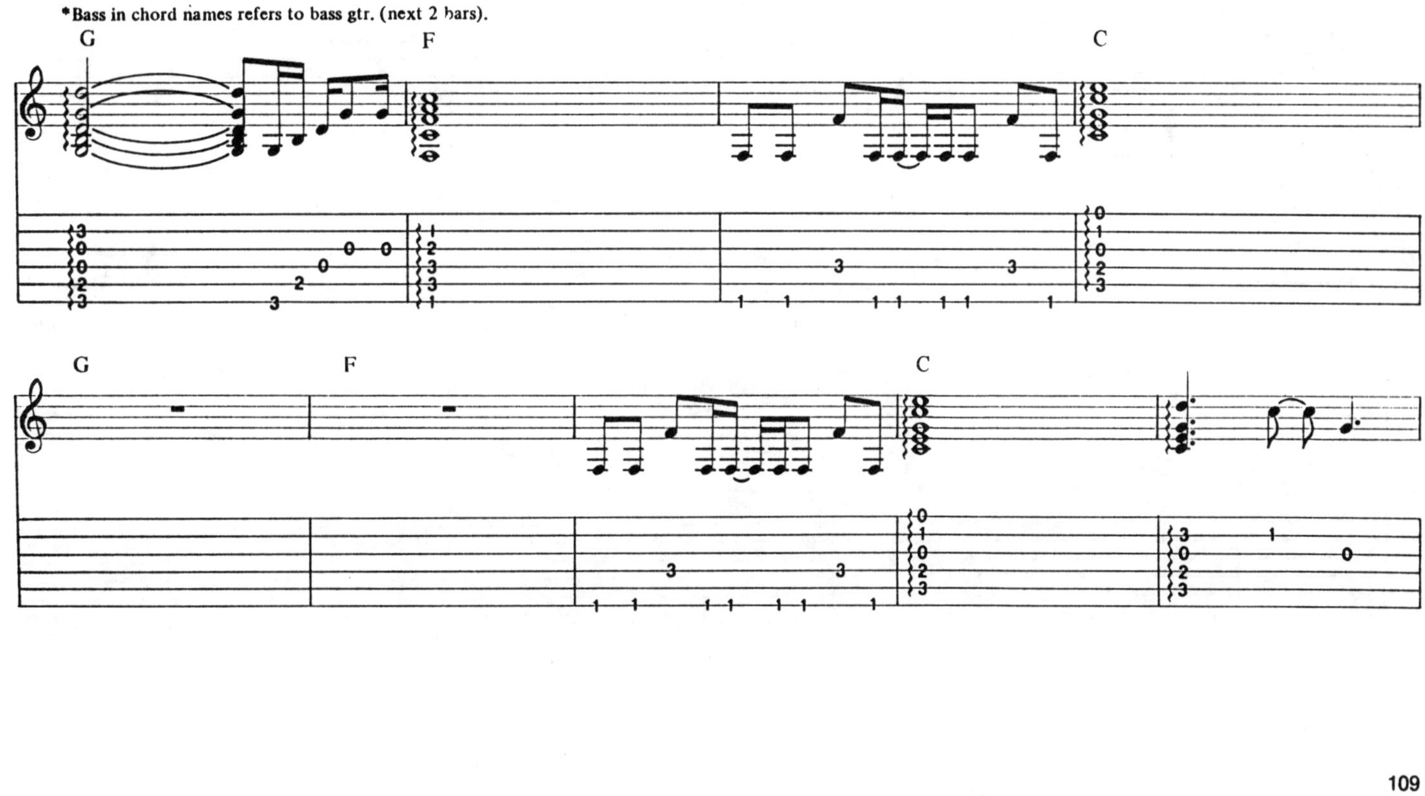

G
F
When I find all of the rea - sons, may - be I'll find_ an - oth - er way, find an - oth -
Rhy. Fig. 1
C
G
F
er day._
With all_ the chang - ing sea - sons_ of my
C
G
F
C
life, may - be I'll get_ it_ right next time._
An now that you've_ been_
(end Rhy. Fig. 1)
G
F
C
bro - ken down,_ got your head_ out_ of_ the clouds,_ you're back down_ on the ground._ And you don't

G F C G F
talk so loud, an you don't walk so proud any-more, and what for?
Guitar solo I
C Am G
Gtr. II
A.H. Full
(15ma)
A.H. pitch: E
(Gtr. III)
F C
Full
H P
sl.

G
F
Full
H
H P
P
C
Well, I jumped in - to the riv -
(Gtr. II out)
w/Rhy. Fig. 1
er too man - y times to make it home. I'm out here on my own, an drift - ing all
a - lone. If it does - n't show, give it time to read be - tween the lines.
Gtr. I
A5
G5
F5
'Cause I see the storm is get - ting clos - er,

A5 G5 F5 G5 A5 G5
and the waves, they get so high.
Seems ev-'ry-thing we've ev-er known's
F5 G5 A5 G5 F5 E D5 C5
here.
Why must it drift a-way and die?
B♭5 A G5 C5
dim.
(Gtr. I out)
B♭ C
Ow! Ah. Ah!
C B♭ C
Gtr. II
Full
w/delay
vol. off
mf
*sim.
*next 6 bars.
Gtr. III
sl.
B♭ C B♭ F
(delay off)
(Gtr. III out)

Guitar solo II
Gtr. I
F5 C5 G5 F5 C5 G5 C5 G5 F5
8va
loco
Full
1/2
H P
w/Rhy. Fill 1
C5
dim.
(Gtr. I out)
I'll nev - er find an - y - one to re -
(Gtr. II out) Gtr. IV
w/chorus
mf
Rhy. Fill 1
Gtr. III

w/Rhy. Fig. 1 (1st 5 bars only)
G F C G
place you. Guess I'll have to make it thru this time, oh, this time
sl.
F C N.C.
Gtr. I
C5 G/B A5 G5
f
with-out you. I knew the storm was get - ting clos -
(Gtr. IV out)
(Gtr. III out)
Gtr. III
*Gtr. IV indicated to right of slash in tab.
F5 G5 A5 G5 F5 G5
er. And all my friends said I was high.
A5 G5 F5 G5 A5 G5 F5
⑥open
E
But ev - 'ry - thing we've ev - er known's here. I nev - er want - ed it to die.
D5 C5
⑥5fr. 3fr. open
A G E
F5
dim.
C
Gtr. III
mf
*Piano arr. for gtr.

YOU COULD BE MINE

(Special Thanks To Bernie Taupin and Elton John)

Words and Music by
Izzy Stradlin' and W. Axl Rose

Gtr. III
Riff A
(w/wah wah)
Gtr. II
Riff A1
Gtr. I
Riff A2
pick slide
P.M.

sl.
1/2
P
Full
1/4
P.M.
rake

(end Riff A)
(end Riff A1)
(end Riff A2)
P.M.
E
Esus4
A5 B5 A5 B5 A5 F♯5 E5
Full
sl.
P
1/4
1/2

F♯5
E5 F♯5 E5 F♯5
A5 B5 A5 B5 A5 F♯5 E5 F♯5
A5 B5 A5 B5 A5 F♯5 E5
Fdbk.
(8va)
Full
Fdbk.
Fdbk. pitch: F♯
Gtr. IV
*Rhy. Fig. 1
P.M.
*Two gtrs. arr. for one gtr.
A5 B5 A5 B5 A5 F♯5 E5 F♯5
1/2
trem. bar
sl.

1st, 2nd Verses
2nd time w/Fill 2
A5 B5 A5 B5 A5 F#5 E5 F#5
Gtr. I
1. I'm a cold heart - break - er, fit ta burn, and I'll rip your heart in two,
2. See additional lyrics
(Gtr. III out)
sl.
Full
P
Gtr. IV tacet 2nd time
(end Rhy. Fig. 1)
Gtr. II
P.M.
P.M.
F5 E5
open
4fr.
F#
and I'll leave you ly - in' on the bed.
Fill 2
1/4
sl.
(w/echo repeat)

F♯5
A5 B5 A5 B5 A5 F♯5 E5 F♯5
A B A B A F♯5 E5
Well, I'll be out the door before ya wake. It's
Gtr. I
P.M.
P.M.
F♯5
A B A B A F♯5 E5
E
nuth - in' new ta you, 'cause I think we've
sl.
sl.
P.M.

A B A B A N.C.
F♯5
A5 B5 A5 B5 A5 N.C.
seen that mov - ie too.
Ow!
'Cause
(cont. in slashes)
1/4 1/2
P.M.
P.M.
P.M.
1/4 1/2
Gtr. I Rhy. Fig. 2A
Chorus
A5
B5
F♯5
you could be mine, but you're
Rhy. Fig. 2
Gtr. II
let ring
let ring
let ring
A5
B5
F♯5
⑤open
A
way out of line. With your
let ring
let ring
P.M.

A5
B5
bitch slap rap - pin' and your co - caine tongue, you get
let ring
let ring
w/Fill 1
F♯5
(end Rhy. Fig. 2A)
sl.
P.M.
A5
nuth - in' done. I said, you
(end Rhy. Fig. 2)
let ring
1. B5
F♯5
A5 B5 A5 B5 A5 F♯5 E5
could be mine. Ow!
(Wow!)
Gtrs. I & II
Fill 1
sl.
sl.

w/Rhy. Fig. 1
Gtr. II
F♯5 E5 F♯5 E5 F♯5 A5 B5 A5 B5 A5 F♯5 E5 F♯5
Fdbk. (15ma)
Fdbk. (15ma)
A5 B5 A5 B5 A5 F♯5 E5
1¼
Fdbk. pitches: F
A E
A5 B5 A5 B5 A5 F♯5 E5 F♯5
A5 B5 A5 B5 A5 F♯5 E5
Now,
Full
1/2
P
2.
B5
C♯5
N.C.
Interlude
w/Riffs A, A1, & A2
N.C.
could be mine!
Gtr. III
P.M.
(w/wah)
sl.
Gtr. II
1/4
Gtr. I
Fdbk. (8va)
Fdbk.
Fdbk. pitch: B

You could be mine.
You could be mine. (Whispered:) Sh - sh - sh - sh - sh. You could be mine.
You could be mine. Sh - sh - sh - sh. You could be mine, mine, mine, mine!
Bridge
Rhy. Fig. 3
(end Rhy. Fig. 3)
w/Rhy. Fig. 3
(Gtrs. I&II)
G5 F♯5 G5 A D A G5
P.M.
Ooh, you've gone sketch-in' too many times. Woo,
F♯5 G5 A5 D A G5
why don't ya give it a rest. Why
F♯5 G5 A B5 A G
5 open
P.M.
must you find
F♯5 D5 A5 B5 D5 A5 B5
Rhy. Fig. 4
Guitar solo
an - oth - er rea - son to cry?
Gtr. III
1/4 1/2 P
let ring
7 7 7 7 7 7 9 (9) 9 9 9 9 9 9 9 9 9 (9) (9) 9 9 (9) (9) 7 7 9 9 7 7 9 7 9 7 9 7 9 9 9 9 9 9 7 7 9 9 9 9 7 7 9 9 7 7

(end Rhy. Fig. 4)
D5 A5
D5 A5 B5
w/Rhy. Fig. 4
A.H. (15ma)
A.H. pitch: D♯
D5 A5 B5
D5 A5
8va
D5 A5 B5
A5 B5
loco
*Both E & A bent w/same finger.
B
C♯
While you're break-in' down my back n' I been rack-in' out my brain, it don't
(Gtr. III out)

Gtr. I
D
④7fr.
A
sl.
(Both gtrs.)
B
mat-ter how we make it 'cause it al - ways ends the same. You can push it for more mile - age but your
Gtr. II
Harm.
*1/2
*Bend neck.
C♯
flaps r' wear - in' thin and I could sleep on it 'til morn-in', but this night-mare nev - er ends, don't for -
get to call my law - yers with ri - dic - u - lous de - mands an you can take the pit - y so far, but it's
Gtr. I
Harm.
(8va)
more than I can stand, 'cause this couch-trip's get - tin' old - er, tell me how long has it been, 'cause
(Both gtrs.)
*Bend neck.

Chorus
w/Rhy. Figs. 2 & 2A
five years is for-ev-er an you have-n't grown up yet.
(Ooh.)
You could be
Gtr. I
mine,
but you're way out of
line.
With your bitch slap rap-pin' and your co-caine tongue, you get
nuth-in' done.
I said, you could be,
Gtr. III
you should be,
you

Outro
w/Rhy. Fig.1 (1st 4 bars only, 4 times)
(type 2)
B5 A5 B5 A5 B5 A5 F#5 E5 F#5 E5 F#5 E5 F#5 A5 B5 A5 B5 A5 F#5 E5
could be mine.
Oh, you could be mine.
M - m - m - mine!
(You could be mine.)
You could be mi - ine.
Ow, you could be mine.
You could be mine.
Ow, you could be mine.
1/4
1/2
Full
8va

Additional Lyrics

2. Now, holidays come, and then they go,
   It's nothin' new today,
   Collect another memory.
   When I come home late at night,
   Don't ask me where I've been.
   Just count your stars I'm home again. *(To Chorus)*

DON'T CRY
(ALT. LYRICS)

Words and Music by
Izzy Stradlin' and W. Axl Rose

w/Fill 1
Am
Dm
G
C
G/B
N.C.
Am7
Dm
No one can live in sor - row,
ask all your friends.
Times that you took in stride, they're
G
C
G/B
N.C.
Am
Dm
G
C
N.C.
back in de-mand.
I was the one who's wash-ing
blood off your hands.
Fill 1
Gtr. II
P
p clean tone w/echo

Chorus
F
G5
Am
Don't you_ cry_ to - night._ I still_ love_ you, ba - by.
(Ooh._
H
*T
*T = thumb
F
G
Am
Don't you_ cry_ to - night._
Ooh._
P
sl.

F G C G/B Am G
Don't you cry to - night. There's a heav - en a - bove you, ba - by.
Ooh. Ooh.)
P
H
F G Am
2nd Verse
w/Fill 2
Am Dm
Gtr. I
And don't you cry to - night.
I know the things you want - ed,
(cont. in slashes)
H
T
Fill 2
Gtr. II
clean tone w/echo
p

G5 (cont. in notation) C G/B N.C. ⑤open A Am Dm
Gtr. I
they're not what you have.
With all the peo - ple talk - in',
Gtrs. I & III
Gtr. III
G5 (cont. in notation) C G/B N.C. ⑤open A Am ④open D Dm Dmsus2 Dm
Gtr. I
it's driv - in' you mad.
If I was stand - ing by you,
Gtr. I & III
Gtr.III
H
G5 (cont. in notation) C G/B N.C. ⑤open A Am ④open D Dm Dmsus2 Dm
Gtr. I
how would you feel
know-ing your love's de - cid - ed,
Gtrs. I & III
Gtr. III
G5 (cont. in notation) C G/B Am G
Chorus
Gtr. I F G5
and all love is real.
An don't you cry to - night.
*(...had, ba - by.)
(Ooh.
Gtrs. I & III
Gtr. III
H
T
*Fade in.

A Am Amsus4 Am F D G D G A
Don't you cry to - night.
Ooh.
Am Amsus4 Am G5 F G D G5
(Gtr. I out)
Don't you cry to - night.
Ooh.
(Gtr. III out)
*Gtr. IV
C5 G/B A5 G5 F5 G5 A5
There's a heav - en a - bove you, ba - by. And don't you cry to - night.
Ooh.)
Gtr. V
A.H.
Full
*Two gtrs. (w/dist.) arr. for one.
Guitar solo
D5 F5 G5 A5 G5 F5 G5
let ring
Full
1/2
1/4

A5
G5
F5
G5
1/4
1/2
Full
H P P
P
sl.
let ring
E5
F5
G5
A5
*P.M.
P.M.
Fdbk.
(Gtr. IV out)
(cont. in Fill 3)
*Play only lowest note of chord when P.M. is indicated (throughout).
Fdbk. pitch.: A
*Vib. applies to bottom note only.
3rd Verse
w/Fill 3
Dm
G
Cadd2
G/B
N.C.
Am
I thought I could live in your world as years all went by.
Gtr. I
mf
Gtr. III
H
Fill 3
Gtr. V
Fdbk.
(8va)
Harm.
3½
trem. bar

Dm G C G/B N.C. Am Dm G
With all the voic-es I've heard, some-thing has died.
And when you're in need of some-one my
Cadd2 G/B N.C. Am Dm G
heart won't de-ny you.
So man-y seem so lone-ly with no one
Gtr. IV C5 G/B A5 G5
left to cry to, ba-by.
(Gtr. III out)

Chorus
F5
G5
A5
P.M.
P.M.-
An don't you cry___ to - night._
(Ooh.___
Ooh.___
H
Gtr. V
Full
3
sl.
A5
F5
G5
C5
G/B
An don't you cry___ to - night._ There's a heav - en a - bove_ you, ba - by._
1/2
P

F5 G5 F5 G5 F5 G5 F5
P.M.
An don't you cry. Don't you ev - er cry. Don't you cry to - night.
Ooh. Ooh, ooh. Ooh.
H
T
Fdbk.
Full
E5 F5 w/Fill 4 G5 F5 G5
P.M.
Ba - by, may - be some - day. And don't you cry. Don't you ev - er cry.
Ooh. Ooh.
Fill 4
Gtr. II
w/distortion
sl.

Free time
w/Fill 5
F5
G5
C5
Don't you cry_ to - night.
rit.
H
Full
rit.
Full
N.C.
sl.
H
Fill 5
Gtr. II
Full
*Swell w/vol. control.

MY WORLD

Words and Music by
W. Axl Rose